A COMEDY IN THREE ACTS

Pillow Talk

Adapted from screenplay by
Stanley Shapiro and Maurice
Richlin which was based on
a story by Russell Rouse and
Clarence Greene. Stage adap-
tation by Christopher Sergel.

THE DRAMATIC PUBLISHING COMPANY

Pillow Talk

A Comedy in Three Acts

FOR SIX MEN, FIFTEEN WOMEN, EXTRAS

CHARACTERS

JAN MORROW...*an interior decorator*
JONATHAN FORBES...*a client*
BRAD ALLEN...*a songwriter*
ALMA...*Jan's maid*
PIEROT ....*Jan's partner*
MRS. WALTERS...*another client*
TONY WALTERS...*her son*
MARIE ⎫
EILEEN ⎬...*Brad's friends*
YVETTE ⎭
MISS CONRAD ⎫
SUPERVISOR ⎬...........................*of the telephone company*
MISS DICKENSON ⎭
POLICEMAN
BESSIE...*Brad's maid*
MRS. FROST ⎫
MRS. AMES ⎬...*prospective clients*
GRAHAM...*a private detective*
GIRL IN CLUB...*a singer*
TILDA ⎫
ANN ⎬...*Jan's assistants*
TELEPHONE OPERATOR (voice only)
MAN (voice only)
STAGE HANDS, GUESTS AT CLUB, ETC.

PLACE: *The apartments of Jan and Brad, New York City.*
TIME: *The present.*

SYNOPSIS

3

CHART OF STAGE POSITIONS

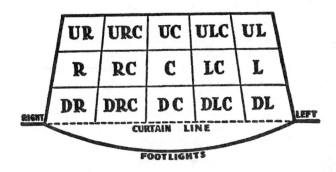

STAGE POSITIONS

Upstage means away from the footlights, *downstage* means toward the footlights, and *right* and *left* are used with reference to the actor as he faces the audience. R means *right*, L means *left*, U means *up*, D means *down*, C means *center*, and these abbreviations are used in combination, as: U R for *up right*, R C for *right center*, D L C for *down left center*, etc. One will note that a position designated on the stage refers to a general territory, rather than to a given point.

NOTE: Before starting rehearsals, chalk off your stage or rehearsal space as indicated above in the *Chart of Stage Positions.* Then teach your actors the meanings and positions of these fundamental terms of stage movement by having them walk from one position to another until they are familiar with them. The use of these abbreviated terms in directing the play saves time, speeds up rehearsals, and reduces the amount of explanation the director has to give to his actors.

PROPERTIES

GENERAL: BRAD'S APARTMENT: Piano and bench, love seat, pillows on love seat, end table, wall mirror, coffee table, telephone. ACT ONE: Empty cup and saucer on piano. ACT TWO: Upright vacuum cleaner behind love seat, file folder; midway in Act Two, coffee things (including cube sugar) on coffee table. ACT THREE: Sport coat on back of chair, cowboy hat beside piano.

JAN'S APARTMENT: Two chairs, small table, sofa, desk, mirror, shelf. ACT ONE: Bright jar on shelf, fabric samples on desk. ACT TWO: Jan's gloves and purse on table. ACT THREE: Small record rack, with record albums.

IN FRONT OF CURTAIN: Telephone, small desk, chair, file folder and other paraphernalia on desk; two small tables and four chairs (St. Regis scene); three small tables and six chairs, crackers and dip on one table (Hidden Door scene).

MISS CONRAD: Telephone.

JAN MORROW: Mail (several letters), wrist watch, brief case, hideous lamp, handkerchief.

JONATHAN FORBES: Key ring and keys, bottle of perfume (gift-wrapped), wrist watch, telephone, bouquet of flowers wrapped in tissue, hideous lamp, ugly chair.

BRAD ALLEN: Pencil, music paper, sport coat, paper (same as Miss Dickenson has earlier in scene), pot of coffee, cup, address book, wrist watch, suit coat, playing cards, key in pocket, telephone.

EILEEN: Telephone, frivolous apron in handbag.

YVETTE: Telephone, attractively wrapped flower box.

ALMA: Empty shopping bag, spray cleaner and rag, vase and unwrapped bouquet, dish and dish towel.

MRS. WALTERS: Small carving wrapped in paper.

MISS DICKENSON: Paper (complaint).

MARIE: Telephone.

BESSIE: Cowboy hat, lariat, and other "western" paraphernalia.

5

GRAHAM: Telephone, brief case containing photograph.
PIEROT: Telephone.

TILDA and ANN: Various decorating items, such as statuary, small rugs and throws, etc., all of them hideous.

STAGEHANDS: Two small tables, four chairs (St. Regis); three small tables, six chairs (The Hidden Door).

AS THE HOUSE LIGHTS DIM, *there is the sound of a telephone being dialed, and then answered.*]

OPERATOR'S VOICE. This is information. May I help you?

JAN'S VOICE. I need information about my party line. You see, every time I try to make a call the *other* party on my line . . .

OPERATOR'S VOICE [*interrupting*]. I'll give you the number to dial for our business office.

JAN'S VOICE [*anxiously*]. This man is on the phone night and day, and when I try to make a call . . .

OPERATOR'S VOICE. Please dial 394-6161-8706-3912.

JAN'S VOICE [*hesitating*]. 3-9-4?

OPERATOR'S VOICE [*faintly exasperated*]. 6161-8706-3912.

[*There is a click as the telephone is hung up, and immediately light is coming up in front of the curtain. At* R, MISS CONRAD, *an executive, is revealed seated at a small desk checking through a folder. At* L, *another young woman* (SUPERVISOR) *wearing a suit uniform, is coming on followed by* JAN MORROW, *an attractive career girl.*]

SUPERVISOR [*is saying pleasantly to* JAN]. Our lobby exhibit this month is called "Your Future Telephone." I expect you noticed the speaker phones, the special intercom systems, telephones that take and give messages—and in a few years we'll have phones you don't even have to dial. All you do is insert a card and . . .

JAN. What about a plain private line?

SUPERVISOR. What about it?

JAN. I'm on a party line.

SUPERVISOR. Yes, I know.

JAN. The only reply I can get out of your business office is a printed form—about your fantastic progress, but meanwhile I should be patient.

SUPERVISOR [*reasonably*]. Then why don't you just——
JAN [*firmly*]. Miss—the other party is *always* talking.
SUPERVISOR. You said that.
JAN. You said you'd take me to the assistant manager.
SUPERVISOR [*gesturing* R]. This way.
JAN [*as she goes, muttering*]. Phones you don't even have to dial . . .
SUPERVISOR [*presenting*]. Miss Conrad . . . this is that Miss Morrow.
MISS CONRAD [*looking up from her desk*]. So *you're* Miss Morrow. [*She riffles the folder in front of her, and* JAN *nods. To* SUPERVISOR.] Thank you, Miss Stevens. [*The* SUPERVISOR *nods and goes out* R.]
JAN [*half apologetic*]. I'm sorry about all those letters, but this has been driving me crazy.
MISS CONRAD [*forcing a smile*]. Miss Morrow—your telephone company wants *everyone* to have a private line. And we're putting in new trunk lines as fast as we can. But with all the construction going on in your area, it takes time. And we have hundreds of applications which take precedence over yours.
JAN [*almost pleading*]. But there must be a way to get one!
MISS CONRAD. Well, if some emergency arose—if you were to get some serious disease, for example—typhoid, smallpox— [*She smiles helpfully.*]—then you'd jump right to the top of our list.
JAN [*hating to be difficult*]. I'm not quite ready for that kind of emergency.
MISS CONRAD. Well, I—I wouldn't know what else to suggest.
JAN. Oh, but I'm at my wit's end—really! You see, I'm an interior decorator and I do a lot of work at home—so naturally there are business calls that I must make—and I cannot get a call through. [*Bitterly.*] That man is always on the phone with some woman.
MISS CONRAD. There's nothing wrong with his being on the phone with . . .

JAN [*cutting in*]. You don't understand.

MISS CONRAD. Understand what?

JAN [*forced to it, confidentially*]. Have you any idea what it's like to be on a party line with a—a—a man so obsessed with women he's practically a—a maniac? [*Startled,* MISS CONRAD *looks around.*]

MISS CONRAD [*leaning forward*]. That's a very serious charge. Can you substantiate it?

JAN. Well, for one thing he's always singing love songs—at all hours—and to different girls. He must have the phone near a piano, and he plays and sings and then talks nonsense—for *hours.*

MISS CONRAD. Has he used objectionable language on the phone?

JAN. No.

MISS CONRAD. Or threats of any nature?

JAN. No.

MISS CONRAD. Has he made immoral overtures to you?

JAN [*confused*]. Well——Oh, not to me!

MISS CONRAD. And you're bothered by this?

JAN. Yes. I mean no! What do you mean—bothered?

MISS CONRAD. You're a single woman, I take it?

JAN. I don't see what that has to do with——

MISS CONRAD. And this man's carrying on with all these other women disturbs you.

JAN [*irked*]. Miss Conrad, please believe me—I don't care what he does. I just want him to stop doing it on my phone!

MISS CONRAD [*with a sigh*]. All right——I'll have one of our inspectors stop by and talk to him.

JAN. Oh, thank you very much.

MISS CONRAD [*meaning to be sympathetic*]. I can see you have a problem.

JAN [*not sure how to take this, speaking firmly*]. With my telephone.

MISS CONRAD. If what you say about this man is true, we may be forced to—disconnect him.

JAN. Good! [*Looking about.*] Which door do I go out? I have to catch a taxi.

MISS CONRAD [*gesturing*]. The way you came.

JAN [*starting* L]. Thank you.

MISS CONRAD. You'll hear from us.

JAN [*calling back*]. I'm counting on it.

[*The light on* MISS CONRAD *dims and she steps off* R. *Meanwhile sounds of street traffic have come up as* JAN *walks* L. *She pauses and calls:*]

JAN. Taxi——taxi! [*An odd horn toots several times, and* JAN *looks* L. *A man is heard calling from off* L.]

JONATHAN'S VOICE. Jan——

[JONATHAN FORBES, *a nattily dressed young businessman, comes on* L, *carrying a key ring.*]

JONATHAN. Jan!

JAN [*smiling*]. Hello, Jonathan.

JONATHAN. Hi. I've got something to tell you.

JAN. Oh?

JONATHAN. I was trying to call you all morning, but your line's been busy.

JAN. Naturally. My life's practically at a standstill.

JONATHAN [*indicating* L]. I just drove that car out of the showroom. How do you like it?

JAN. It's marvelous. Funny-sounding horn, too.

JONATHAN. Mercedes-Benz 300 SL Roadster. Like the color?

JAN. It's beautiful.

JONATHAN [*as they move* L, *looking*]. The upholstery?

JAN. Perfect.

JONATHAN [*holding up keys*]. It's yours. [*He drops the keys into her hand. She looks down at the keys, then up to* JONATHAN *again.*]

JAN. Huh?

JONATHAN. In grateful appreciation of the brilliant job you

did redecorating my office.

JAN. What? [*Laughing.*] Why, Jonathan . . . Jonathan, you just don't go around giving girls Mercedes-Benzes.

[*A* POLICEMAN *is coming on* L.]

JONATHAN. I do.

POLICEMAN. That your car, mac?

JONATHAN. No, officer, it's hers.

JAN. Oh!

POLICEMAN. That your car, miss?

JAN. No, it's his. Jonathan——Jonathan, you're very sweet and very generous, but I cannot accept a gift like that.

JONATHAN. Why not?

JAN. Well, it's—it's too personal.

JONATHAN. That?

JAN. Yes.

JONATHAN. If I gave you—perfume, if I gave you lingerie—*that* would be personal. But—but a car!

POLICEMAN [*gruffly*]. Come on, mac. If it's yours—move it.

JAN [*giving back the keys*]. Here—send me the perfume.

JONATHAN [*reproving*]. You shouldn't reject me like that. Suppose I turn out to be your last chance?

JAN [*smiling*]. Don't *you* start. The phone company just got through acting as though I were some sort of crank spinster.

JONATHAN. Can I drop in later—about interior decorating?

POLICEMAN. Mac!

JAN [*starting* L]. We could use more business. [*Calling off.*] Taxi!

JONATHAN [*calling after her as she goes out* L]. Listen—are you *sure* you don't want the car?

JAN [*off* L]. Yes, I'm sure. See you later. [JONATHAN *and the* POLICEMAN *look after her for a moment.*]

JONATHAN [*shrugging*]. All right, officer, I'll move it. [*Shakes his head.*] My analyst will never believe this.

POLICEMAN [*shaking his head, too*]. Neither will mine. [*They go off* L. *A piano somewhere is heard being played casually by someone picking out a melody line.*]

THE CURTAIN RISES, *revealing the set, which consists of two sections, both of them well upstage. The right section suggests a small masculine apartment and it occupies about one-third of the width of the stage. There is a small piano along the wall* R, *a love seat and an end table on which the telephone belongs, though at the moment it has been set on top of the piano with the receiver off. The other two-thirds of the stage is deserted at the moment. It is separated by a portion of wall from the other part of the set. The separation should be definite enough so that it is clear that these are two different apartments. The left apartment has two chairs, a small table, a sofa, and a desk. Just as the right apartment is masculine, the left apartment is feminine. At rise of curtain the emphasis of the lights is at the right where* BRAD, *a handsome man in sport clothes, is at the piano playing the melody line heard earlier.* BRAD *comes to the end of a phrase in the music, and leans forward to speak into the telephone, saying the girl's name as though it were a part of the song.*]

BRAD [*into the telephone*]. Eileen——Eileen!

[*A sophisticated girl wearing high-fashion clothes steps on at extreme* D L, *languidly holding a telephone, the cord of which leads off* L.]

EILEEN [*into telephone*]. Brad—darling. [*He picks up the receiver from the piano.*] Brad——
BRAD. Yes?
EILEEN. I love you.
BRAD. I know.
EILEEN. I just had to call you. I'll never forget last night, especially when you sang me your new song.
BRAD. *Our* song, Eileen. I wrote it for you.

[JAN *is coming into the apartment at* L, *taking off her gloves and looking through the mail she's brought up.*]

EILEEN [*going on, sighing*]. Oh, Brad! Would you sing it to
me again?

BRAD [*faintly pained*]. *Again?*

EILEEN [*a plea*]. Hum a little?

BRAD. We don't really have the lyrics yet, anyway, but *you* know
the name that fits——[JAN *has put down the mail, and
purposefully she picks up the telephone.*]

EILEEN [*continuing*]. Oh—*Brad!*

BRAD [*resigned*]. Here we go again——

JAN [*dismayed*]. Not again! [*Both* BRAD *and* EILEEN *react to*
JAN'S *voice. However the interruption doesn't stop* BRAD,
who goes right on. NOTE: *None of the telephone conversa-
tions actually go through a sound system. The telephones are
held, and the characters speak as though into them in their
regular stage voices.*]

BRAD [*into telephone, firmly*]. Our song goes like this, dear——
[*With one hand,* BRAD *fingers out the tune on the piano,
while he holds the telephone with the other hand, humming
along into it.*]

EILEEN. Oh, that's beautiful.

JAN [*cutting in*]. I do hate to interrupt, but would you mind
hanging up, please?

EILEEN [*into telephone, casually*]. Brad . . . who is that?

BRAD. The other half of my party line. Just ignore her. She'll
go away.

JAN [*indignantly*]. You were on this phone when I went out
an hour ago—and you're *still* on it! I have an important call
to make.

BRAD. I happen to consider this an important call.

JAN. Humming to a girl in the middle of the day?

EILEEN. It's none of your business what he does to me! Or
when!

JAN. Would you *please* get off this line—for just a few minutes?

BRAD. No.

JAN. Oh! [*As his humming begins again, she hangs up sharply, stares at the telephone furiously, and then takes out her anger in the way she opens and then throws away her mail.*]

BRAD [*completing the musical phrase again*]. Eileen——Eileen. [*A bit businesslike.*] That's it, dear. I've a lot of composing to do. I don't have any of the music over to the orchestrator yet and the producer plans to put the new musical into rehearsal in four weeks.

EILEEN. You work too hard.

BRAD. Not recently.

EILEEN. Can I call you later?

BRAD. Oh, all right.

EILEEN. See you——[*She hangs up and steps back off* L. BRAD *picks up a pencil and in a more businesslike fashion starts fingering out a tune and marking notes on some music paper on the piano in front of him.* JAN *finishes opening mail and then turns back to her telephone.*]

JAN [*considering telephone, then giving up*]. Oh, what's the use. [*She turns and goes out into her kitchen. At this moment, in Brad's apartment, the telephone rings and* BRAD *puts down his pencil and picks up the receiver.*]

BRAD [*into telephone*]. Hello——

[*Another sophisticated girl, this one wearing a bright sweater and toreador pants, steps on at extreme* D R. *She is holding a telephone, the cord of which leads off* R.]

YVETTE [*into telephone*]. I know it's early, *cherie*, but I just had to talk to you. Will I see you tonight?

BRAD. I'm sorry, Yvette. I have to work.

YVETTE [*disappointed*]. Oh.

BRAD. I still have six songs to write for the new show.

YVETTE. But you will have to go out and eat dinner, no?

BRAD. I'll throw something together here.

YVETTE. No, darling, you mustn't! You must keep up your strength. I'll come over and cook something for you, yes?

BRAD. Make it next Tuesday.

YVETTE. Oh, thank you, darling.

BRAD. It's nothing.

YVETTE. Brad?

BRAD. Um-hm?

YVETTE. Sing me a little of our song?

BRAD [*chuckling*]. Yvette——

YVETTE. Please——

BRAD [*with a sigh*]. Oh, all right. [*With the telephone in his left hand, he starts picking out the identical tune he played before.*]

[*In the other apartment, JAN comes back in from the kitchen with a list she's just made, and she gets set by the telephone to call someone about it. She picks up the telephone just as BRAD finishes the musical phrase.*]

BRAD [*into telephone, as before*]. Yvette—Yvette!

YVETTE [*melting*]. *Cherie!*

JAN [*into telephone, exasperated*]. I've got to make a call. Now will you please get off this phone?

YVETTE [*casually*]. Who is that woman?

BRAD. Some little eavesdropper on my party line.

JAN [*exploding*]. Eavesdropper!

BRAD. Probably some spinster crank.

JAN [*stung, out of breath*]. Spinster crank!

BRAD. She's *always* listening in. That's how she brightens up her drab, empty life.

JAN [*still crushed, but partially collecting herself*]. If I could get a call through once in a while, my life wouldn't be so drab! [*With this, JAN hangs up. She stares at the telephone with dismay, and the memory of the comment makes her bite her lip.*]

BRAD. I'm just taking time now for a quick cup of instant coffee, then back to work.

YVETTE. But I get to see you Tuesday?

BRAD. Sure.

YVETTE. *Au revoir, cherie.*

BRAD. 'By——[*He hangs up, makes another note on the music*

paper, then picks up the empty cup and saucer from on top of the piano and goes out into his kitchen. Meanwhile JAN *has crossed to look at herself in a mirror, inspecting herself. Her bell rings, and without turning she calls:*]

JAN. It's open, Alma. Come in.

[ALMA, *a wry and witty by-the-day houseworker, comes in. She's dressed in working clothes and carries an empty shopping bag.*]

ALMA. How did you know it was me?

JAN. Who else could it be?

ALMA. It could be your big spender boy friend—you know, you decorated his office.

JAN. Jonathan——[*Humorously.*] That nice idiot is starting to talk as though he's my last chance.

ALMA [*curiously*]. Are you starting to worry about that already?

JAN [*smiling*]. I *started* when I was twelve. Then I grew up, moved to New York—and I've been too busy to give the subject another thought.

ALMA. I better get on with the cleaning. [*Moving* U L.] I'll start with the kitchen. [*Her curiosity makes her pause. Casually.*] Anything *special* happen this morning?

JAN. No. [*Nods toward kitchen.*] There's some new shelving paper for the cupboards, and when the laundry man comes, the bag is just inside the closet.

ALMA. Sure.

JAN [*defensively*]. The *only* thing that happened——I met Jonathan on the street and he made a fool of himself. [*Gestures toward telephone.*] And our party-line Casanova was even more sickening than usual.

ALMA [*meaning to be sympathetic*]. He really bothers you.

JAN [*sharply*]. Because he ties up the telephone.

ALMA. That's what I meant.

JAN [*exasperated*]. I don't know why all the men in this town are so infantile!

ALMA [*reasonably*]. You haven't seen all of them yet.

JAN. There's a Manhattan type, and the biggest thing on their minds is getting a front table at the restaurant all the other Manhattan types are going to this week.

ALMA. Wherever you go you'll find men who——

JAN. Will you find them spending the whole day humming to girls over the telephone?

ALMA [*conceding*]. You've got me there.

JAN [*emphatically*]. The more I see of these characters, the happier I am that I'm single.

ALMA. Yes, ma'am. [*There is a knock on the door.*]

JAN. I'll get it.

ALMA [*pausing at kitchen door*]. The trouble with the sort of man *you* want—I don't think you'll find one any closer than the backwoods part of Australia.

JAN [*ruefully*]. I'm beginning to think you're right. [*As she crosses to door, smiling.*] Maybe that's where I should take my next vacation.

[ALMA *smiles back and exits to kitchen. As* JAN *opens the door* L, PIEROT, *an elegantly dressed but very nervous young man, hurries in.*]

PIEROT. Oh, Jan—thank heaven you're here.

JAN. I had an errand, and then I came back to sort over some fabric samples.

PIEROT. Jan—that woman is going to drive me *out* of my mind. Has she come yet?

JAN. What woman?

PIEROT. Now she wants Ming Dynasty in the rumpus room.

JAN [*realizing*]. Mrs. Walters.

PIEROT. She has the taste of a water buffalo.

JAN [*a rhetorical question*]. Then why do business with her?

PIEROT [*conceding*]. Because she happens to be a very rich water buffalo.

JAN [*smiling with him*]. Exactly.

PIEROT. She said she wanted to look in at one of those primitive art places, then she was coming to see what you've picked out for her drapes.

JAN. I better have Alma fix some fresh coffee. [*There is a knock on the door.*]

PIEROT. Oh, dear.

JAN. If that's Mrs. Walters, stall her a few minutes while I get things ready.

PIEROT [*unhappily*]. I can't bear being left alone with that appalling woman.

JAN [*shortly*]. If she had impeccable taste, she wouldn't have any use for us, would she?

PIEROT [*with grudging admiration*]. All you ever think about, Jan—*business*.

JAN [*irked*]. Answer the door. [*She goes out into the kitchen. PIEROT gives a "What'd I say?" shrug as he opens the door.*]

PIEROT [*forcing a broad smile, effusively*]. Mrs. Walters—we meet again.

[MRS. WALTERS, *a stylish and wealthy woman who doesn't take much seriously, comes in carrying an object wrapped in paper.*]

MRS. WALTERS. Since your partner doesn't come to the office, I've come here.

PIEROT. She uses this as an office, too.

MRS. WALTERS. There doesn't seem to be any communication between the two places.

PIEROT. We could use a switchboard. [*Noticing.*] You've been shopping.

MRS. WALTERS [*putting it aside*]. We'll wait for Jan.

PIEROT [*calling into kitchen*]. Jan!

MRS. WALTERS [*picking up a bright jar*]. Is this that expensive vase you bought for me?

PIEROT [*gasping*]. Be careful! It's priceless!

MRS. WALTERS. Really? What is it?

PIEROT [*importantly*]. A fourteenth-century crematory urn.

MRS. WALTERS. A crematory urn? [*Smiling.*] Is anybody in it?

PIEROT. Not at the moment.

MRS. WALTERS [*giggling*]. That's good. Then we can drill a hole in the bottom without anyone running out.

PIEROT. A hole?

MRS. WALTERS. So we can wire it for a lamp.

PIEROT [*taking urn back and replacing it on shelf*]. Mrs. Walters——[*Struggling to keep his temper.*] We do *not* wire fourteenth-century crematory urns!

[JAN *is coming back in from kitchen.*]

MRS. WALTERS. I suppose not.

PIEROT. And furthermore——

JAN [*cutting in as she enters*]. Furthermore, we'll hide a light in the ceiling that will display your vase *dramatically*—and at the same time give you as much illumination as a lamp.

MRS. WALTERS [*pleased*]. You solve everything, Jan.

JAN. I'm sorry I wasn't at the office to meet you.

MRS. WALTERS. That's all right, dear. Mr. Pierot and I had a very fruitful morning. Didn't we, Mr. P.?

PIEROT. Very fruitful.

JAN. You've been shopping?

MRS. WALTERS [*opening package*]. Something I picked out myself. [*She has unwrapped a nonsensical "primitive" carving.*] There! I thought it would go wonderfully well with——

JAN [*gently firm*]. I'm afraid that's the last thing you need in a quiet suburb like Scarsdale, Mrs. Walters.

MRS. WALTERS. Oh? Why?

JAN. It's a fertility goddess.

MRS. WALTERS [*looking at it again, startled*]. Oh, my dear! I had no idea!

JAN [*tactfully*]. It's our job to help you with these things.

MRS. WALTERS [*faintly wounded*]. I wanted you to meet me at the shop, but I couldn't reach you.

JAN [*grimly*]. I've been having difficulty.

MRS. WALTERS. I called six or seven times.

JAN. Let's have a cup of coffee, and then look at some of the drapery samples.

MRS. WALTERS. All right. [*Glancing regretfully at carving.*] When my son picks me up he can take the—goddess back to the store.

JAN [*gesturing toward kitchen*]. It's all ready out here.

MRS. WALTERS [*as she takes her eyes away from the carving, humorously*]. Savage little thing, isn't it? [*She goes out into kitchen.*]

PIEROT. I'm going back to the office. [*Hushed.*] That woman!

JAN [*smiling*]. The best kind of water buffalo.

PIEROT. I'll call you later. [*Amending.*] At least, I'll try.

JAN. Lover boy got started early today.

PIEROT. There *must* be a way to get a private line. [*An idea dawning.*] Why don't you tell them it's an emergency?

JAN [*sourly*]. Thank you, Mr. P.

PIEROT. But you have to do *something!*

JAN. I spent the morning at the telephone company. I reported the entire situation.

PIEROT. It's about time.

JAN. I'm getting some action. They're sending out an inspector.

PIEROT [*crossing to door*]. Finally.

JAN [*grimly*]. And as far as I'm concerned—whatever lover boy gets, he has coming!

PIEROT [*with relief*]. You finally fixed him. Then I will call later. [*He goes out. JAN pauses, reaches out and pats her telephone.*]

JAN [*with pardonable vehemence*]. A little something you didn't quite expect, lover boy. [*Calling ahead to kitchen.*] Right with you, Mrs. Walters. [*JAN goes out into kitchen. At the other side of the stage, there is a knocking on the door to Brad's apartment.*]

BRAD [*off R, calling*]. Be right there—just a minute.

[*BRAD comes in, in the process of slipping into a sport coat.*]

BRAD [*calling*]. Who is it?

MISS DICKENSON [*from outside*]. Telephone company.

[*BRAD opens the door. MISS DICKENSON, a pretty young inspec-*

tor from the telephone company, is standing there.]

MISS DICKENSON [*impressed*]. Mr. Allen?

BRAD. Yes?

MISS DICKENSON. I'm from the telephone——

BRAD. Well, hello . . . come in.

MISS DICKENSON [*stepping inside, decidedly aware of* BRAD]. I—uh—I'm, uh—I'm Miss Dickenson. I'm an inspector.

BRAD [*puzzled*]. Well, what would you like to inspect?

MISS DICKENSON. You. Oh, I mean, uh—we've received a complaint about you.

BRAD. Oh?

MISS DICKENSON [*holding up paper*]. It's this.

BRAD [*smiling, with charm*]. Well, I—I've never had any complaints before. [*He reaches gently for the paper, but she is putting it back.*]

MISS DICKENSON. I wouldn't think so——[*Flustered.*] Well, what I mean——

BRAD. That paper about the complaint—I suppose it's confidential?

MISS DICKENSON. Oh, yes.

BRAD. I was just going out for a breath of air. Would you like to come for a walk with me?

MISS DICKENSON. But the reason I——

BRAD. We could discuss the whole situation—everything.

MISS DICKENSON [*half helpless*]. I guess I should hear your side of it.

BRAD [*looking into her eyes, his voice low*]. That's all I'm asking.

MISS DICKENSON. I *do* want to be fair.

BRAD. It isn't often you meet someone who feels that way.

MISS DICKENSON. Well, after all—I mean, that's the Bill of Rights.

BRAD. I happen to be a composer, and I'm working on a song about a girl—only I don't know what name to give her! [*They are in the process of going.*] I was wondering—what's *your* first name?

[*As they complete their exit* R, *at the other side of the stage in Jan's apartment,* JAN *is coming out from the kitchen.*]

JAN [*calling back as she comes in*]. Since your son isn't here yet, there's time to show you some of the other materials.

MRS. WALTERS [*calling from kitchen*]. Jan——You don't suppose my son could have been calling, but couldn't get through? [JAN *has crossed to desk and is busy sorting through drapery samples.*]

JAN [*calling back*]. Would you pick up the extension phone there in the breakfast nook? See if anyone is on the line. [*She finds the particular fabric she wanted.*] Ah.

MRS. WALTERS [*from kitchen*]. No—no one on it.

[ALMA *is coming in from the kitchen.*]

ALMA [*aside to* JAN]. Imagine that!

JAN [*a bit proud of herself, to* ALMA]. Well, well, well! [JAN *goes back out.* ALMA *looks after her as she continues to cross. As she turns, she's looking directly at the primitive carving.*]

ALMA [*jumping*]. Oh! [*Then she collects herself, leans forward, squinting at it, puzzled.*] Hat rack? Glove drier? [*Shrugs. The answer.*] Back scratcher.

[*She is interrupted by a knock on the door, which she opens.* TONY WALTERS, *a college boy, enters.*]

TONY. This the interior decorating place?

ALMA. In a way—yes.

TONY [*looking about with disapproval*]. I could've guessed.

ALMA [*faintly indignant*]. You selling subscriptions to something?

TONY [*startled*]. Me? [*Irked.*] I'm looking for my mother. [*Briefly.*] Is Mrs. Walters here?

ALMA. Just a moment——[*Calls out* U L, *pleasantly.*] Someone out here looking for his mother.

TONY. Now look! [*Getting her straight.*] I'm in my fourth year at Harvard.

ALMA. I'll bet that takes a *lot* of subscriptions.

[MRS. WALTERS *is coming in* U L.]

TONY [*continuing to* ALMA, *furiously*]. If you're such a hot interior decorator—[*Pointing to primitive carving.*]—what are you doing with a piece of junk like this?

MRS. WALTERS. Junk?

TONY. I don't like to say anything, Mother, but you should get a different decorator.

MRS. WALTERS [*flatly*]. Why?

TONY [*holding up the carving, with amused contempt*]. Anyone with the miserable taste to pick out *this* atrocity!

MRS. WALTERS. Tony——

TONY [*laughing at it*]. What it looks like to me—a back scratcher!

ALMA [*cheerfully*]. And that's after three years at Harvard!

MRS. WALTERS [*with asperity*]. One more remark, Tony, and you'll get that as your graduation present.

[JAN *is coming in* U L.]

TONY [*muttering*]. I still say you should have a *modern* decorator. This phony primitive—it could only be picked out by a has-been.

MRS. WALTERS. Thank you.

TONY. But honestly——

MRS. WALTERS. Tony, *I* picked it out.

TONY [*swallowing*]. Oh.

MRS. WALTERS [*introducing*]. And this is my old-fashioned decorator, Jan Morrow.

JAN [*pleasantly*]. Don't get around much any more.

TONY [*startled*]. But if you're——[*Turns to* ALMA.] Then who are——

JAN. She's Chairman of the Board.

ALMA. The business before the Board right now is shelving paper.

TONY [*a half apology*]. I didn't realize——

ALMA [*patting his shoulder as she passes*]. Harvard still has a few months with you. I just hope they don't get discouraged. [ALMA *goes out* U L.]

MRS. WALTERS. I don't know whether Tony's worse than most, or whether they're all like that.

TONY [*pained*]. Are you about ready?

MRS. WALTERS [*to* JAN]. You're right about the fabric—the drapes *should* be neutral.

JAN [*explaining*]. Otherwise they'll clash with your paintings.

MRS. WALTERS. You *are* coming to my supper party tonight at the St. Regis?

JAN [*hesitatingly*]. I wasn't sure——

MRS. WALTERS. You should meet some of these people—and Tony can see you home.

TONY [*pleased at the prospect*]. Hey——

JAN. But I didn't hear, and I thought——

MRS. WALTERS. I kept calling to confirm, last night, till the busy signal was driving me out of my mind.

JAN. Of course I'll come—and I'm very grateful.

MRS. WALTERS. You're doing a wonderful job, and it *should* lead to more business. [*Hesitates.*] If I want to reach you later——

JAN. Just give me a call. The telephone situation is well in hand.

MRS. WALTERS. Good. Come along, Tony. And bring the—the atrocity. [MRS. WALTERS *goes out* L.]

TONY [*pausing at door, to* JAN]. See ya later. [TONY *gives her a slight leer, then he goes out.* JAN *lets out a slight sigh. Her eyes are drawn to the telephone. She crosses back to it, and a little nervously picks up the receiver. A look of bliss comes over her face as she hears the dial tone, and she replaces the receiver.*]

JAN [*to herself, with satisfaction*]. Well in hand! [*She picks up a fabric sample, and turns it over to check number. Reading.*] Antique silk, burnt gold number 44——[*She is interrupted by her telephone ringing, and she reaches out and*

picks up receiver.] Burnt gold number——[*Into telephone.*]
Hello——

[MISS CONRAD *steps on* D R, *holding a telephone in her hand.*]

MISS CONRAD. This is Miss Conrad of the telephone company.
   Is this Miss Morrow?

JAN. Oh, yes.

MISS CONRAD. I marked your complaint for immediate attention,
   and I've just this minute received the report from the inspector.

JAN. Yes, well?

MISS CONRAD. In view of the fuss you made, I wanted to call at
   once. [*Sharply.*] Your complaint has been found completely
   unwarranted and untruthful.

JAN [*stunned*]. *What!*

MISS CONRAD. The report from our inspector, Miss Dickenson,
   is quite definite.

JAN. *Miss* Dickenson? You sent a *woman?*

MISS CONRAD. She's a qualified inspector.

JAN [*horrified*]. But that's like sending a marshmallow to put
   out a bonfire!

MISS CONRAD [*coldly*]. You regard the person sharing your
   party line as a—*bonfire?*

JAN [*getting angry*]. I regard him as the most inconsiderate,
   infantile, idiotic——

MISS CONRAD [*cutting in*]. I don't think the telephone company
   is equipped to solve—whatever your problem seems to be——

JAN [*interrupting, furious*]. Now you look here——

MISS CONRAD [*flatly*]. We're closing this file. Our inspector
   found him extremely cooperative.

JAN. I'll just bet he was! [*She slams down the telephone.* MISS
   CONRAD *also hangs up and steps back off* D R. JAN *clenches
   her fists in furious frustration, but she doesn't know how to
   let it out. She slams about the room.*] Oh! Oh!

[*Meanwhile* BRAD *has breezed back into his apartment, carrying
the paper* MISS DICKENSON *wasn't going to let him see. He*

crosses to telephone, glances at paper, and then dials number.
BRAD *is humming to himself with a satisfied smile on his face
as he waits for call. The telephone rings in Jan's apartment
and she snatches it up.*]

JAN [*sharply*]. Hello! [BRAD *winces away from the telephone
as though his ear were hurt.* JAN *gets herself together and
speaks in a more reasonable tone.*] Hello?

BRAD [*into telephone*]. Miss Morrow? [*Glancing at paper.*]
Miss Jan Morrow?

JAN. Yes?

BRAD. My name is Brad Allen.

JAN [*without curiosity*]. Brad Allen—yes?

BRAD. I've been advised by the phone company that there's a code
number for our party line.

JAN [*doing take*]. *Our* party line? So *you're*——

BRAD. The code number is seven-nine-three. Now—if you have
any future complaints to make, I suggest you dial it and
complain to me personally.

JAN [*bitterly*]. Why, Mr. Allen—if I hadn't complained, the
inspector would never have found out how—uh, cooperative
you are.

BRAD [*sharply*]. Miss Morrow—why are you so fascinated with
my personal affairs?

JAN. Not fascinated, Mr. Allen. Revolted!

BRAD. You don't see me going down to the phone company
complaining about your affairs.

JAN. I have none to complain about.

BRAD. It figures.

JAN. What do you mean—it figures?

BRAD. Well, obviously you're a woman who lives alone and
doesn't like it.

JAN. I happen to like living alone!

BRAD. Look, I don't know *what's* bothering you, but don't try
to take your problems out on me.

JAN. I have no problems. There isn't *anything* that bothers
me——

BRAD. I see.

JAN [*with dignity*]. I don't know what you see, Mr. Allen—
but let's try to be adult about this and—and work out some
sort of schedule where I can make my business calls and you
can make your—whatever you call the calls you make. [BRAD
is smiling as he listens.] Now—from the hour to the half
hour the phone will be yours. From the half-hour to the hour
it will be mine. Should either of us receive a call during the
other's half hour, he—or she—will terminate the conversation as quickly as possible. In emergencies, each will exercise
a little tolerance. How does that sound?

BRAD. Like a report from the United Nations.

JAN. You mean you disagree?

BRAD. No, it might work.

JAN. Well, I hope so! I understand that we're going to have
to share this party line for at least another month. We'll just
have to try getting along with each other——[*Sighs.*]

BRAD. Well?

JAN. I was waiting for you to make some off-color remark!

BRAD. Miss Morrow, is that all you have on your mind?

JAN. Never mind my mind! You stick to your half-hour and
I'll stick to my half-hour! [*She hangs up, as does* BRAD, *who
is vastly amused. He is taking off his sport coat as he goes out
into his kitchen.*]

[ALMA, *meanwhile, is coming back in from Jan's kitchen.*]

ALMA. You know, he makes pretty good sense.

JAN. Were you listening on the extension again?

ALMA. Yes, ma'am.

JAN. Alma, have you no shame?

ALMA. No, ma'am. He's brightened up many a dreary afternoon
for me.

JAN. What did he say that made such good sense?

ALMA. If there's anything worse than a woman living alone, it's
a woman saying she likes it.

JAN. Well, I do like it! I have a good job—a lovely apartment—

I go out to the best places—the theatre, the finest restaurants
——Well, what am I missing?

ALMA. When you have to ask, believe me—you're missing
something.

JAN. What is a girl supposed to do? Go out in the street and
look for the right sort of man—and then just ask him to
marry her?

ALMA. No, don't do that. It won't work.

JAN. Of course not! And from what I've seen of the men
around here, I'll keep right on waiting, thank you. I'm *glad*
to take my chances.

ALMA. You're getting touchy.

JAN. I am *not* getting——[*Stops herself and smiles.*] You're
right. I'm getting touchy. It's been one of those days. [*There's
a knock on her door.*]

ALMA. Maybe there's Galahad now.

JAN [*crossing to door, smiling*]. I'll settle for that honest backwoods Australian.

[JONATHAN *is revealed when she opens the door. He sounds
his own fanfare and steps in holding out a gift package with
a big ribbon around it.*]

JONATHAN. Ta—da! [*Presenting gift package.*] I brought you
the perfume. Chanel number—something. [*Shrugs.*] I've no
head for figures.

JAN [*lightly*]. Does the word "kangaroo" suggest anything?

JONATHAN [*brightly*]. Lightweight shoes. There's an English
bootmaker on Madison near Seventieth, and he uses——

ALMA [*going out* U L]. Wrong answer—you lose.

JONATHAN [*admiring* JAN]. You look beautiful. What'd I
lose?

JAN [*amused*]. Nothing important. Now, is there something
you want decorated?

JONATHAN. Yes—my future. Jan, why don't you marry me?

JAN [*touched*]. Jonathan—you're doing wonders for my
morale. But I don't love you.

JONATHAN. Well, that's absurd!

JAN. Oh?

JONATHAN [*frankly*]. I'm young, I'm rich, I'm healthy, I'm good-looking——[*Glances in her mirror.*] I'm *very* good-looking. I've got everything.

JAN. Including three ex-wives!

JONATHAN. Oh, that's what it is!

JAN. I don't mean to be stuffy——

JONATHAN. Please don't hold that against me! Those marriages were just a revolt against my mother. I'm trying to work it out. I'm trying to find out why I dislike her so. I've been talking to this psychiatrist about my mother for two years now.

JAN. And?

JONATHAN. It's perfectly healthy. He dislikes her as much as I do. And he's from Vienna!

JAN [*smiling*]. No matter how well adjusted you are, I still——

JONATHAN [*cutting in, eagerly*]. This time it'll be different, Jan. You'll see. We'll go to Mexico. It'll be like starting from scratch. I've never been married in Mexico.

JAN. I just don't happen to love you.

JONATHAN. How do you know? Love isn't an opinion. It's— it's a chemical reaction. We've never even kissed.

JAN [*holding up her face*]. All right—let's check it out. [*There is a gentle kiss; they break, and* JAN *looks at him soberly.*]

JONATHAN [*defensively*]. Well, they didn't hit the moon with the first missile-shot, either.

JAN [*giggling*]. Oh, Jonathan. I guess that's what I want—to hit the moon.

JONATHAN. I'll tell you what——

JAN. Hm?

JONATHAN. I have to see someone—about that show I'm helping produce—but it's practically next door. I could stop in here on my way back, and we could go out for dinner, and— well, try another count-down.

JAN. Can't do it. One of our clients asked me to come to a party she's having at the St. Regis.

JONATHAN. Then I'll call you tomorrow—if I can ever get through the busy signal.

[*In the other apartment, meanwhile,* BRAD *comes back in from the kitchen carrying a coffee pot and cup which he puts purposefully on the piano, sits down, and starts fingering out a melody and then writing down the notes on music paper.*]

JAN. Oh, call between the half-hour and the hour.

JONATHAN. How come?

JAN. I've signed a cease-fire with my party line.

JONATHAN [*pausing at the door*]. Jan, marry me and I'll smother you with private phones.

JAN. You'd better leave. That kind of talk can sweep a girl off her feet!

JONATHAN [*humorously*]. Ten—nine—eight—seven——

JAN [*pushing him out*]. Go audition a bunch of dazzling beauties for your new show.

JONATHAN [*ruefully*]. I never seem to get to that part. All I do is sign checks made out to various unions. Have a terrible time at the St. Regis. [JAN *closes the door after* JONATHAN, *then leans back against it, considering. She smiles affectionately and shakes her head. In the other apartment* BRAD *is irritated at his lack of progress. He takes a big drink of coffee, then goes back to trying to find the right melody line, hitting the notes harder.* JAN *regards the gift package of perfume.*]

JAN [*picking up package, calling off*]. Alma—would you like a little perfume?

ALMA [*off* U L]. I was planning to help myself.

JAN. Oh. [*Considers package; with disapproval.*] I wonder what kind of a man is actually attracted by this sort of thing?

ALMA [*off* U L]. The government should make them put that information on the bottle. [JAN *smiles at this and is putting package back on table. In the other apartment,* BRAD *gets up from the piano, starts to go into the other room, but pauses as he sees telephone and considers.* JAN, *meanwhile, looks at her watch and then turns to consider her telephone.*]

BRAD [*to himself*]. Maybe I need a little inspiration——[*He starts looking through an address book.*]

JAN [*calling*]. Alma—I'm going to test the new system.

ALMA [*off* U L]. What system?

BRAD [*continuing to himself, considering number in his book*]. Maybe Marie.

JAN [*calling back to* ALMA]. For dividing up the telephone. [BRAD *picks up the telephone and, referring back to his book, starts dialing.* JAN *checks her watch again, picks up her telephone.*] I'll astound my office with a call. [*She puts the telephone to her ear and reaches out to dial. She does a take as she realizes that* BRAD *is dialing. Sharply.*] Mr. Allen—Mr. Allen!

BRAD [*putting telephone to his ear, with charm*]. Hello . . . Marie?

JAN [*shortly*]. This is Miss Morrow.

BRAD [*startled*]. What?

JAN. Mr. Allen, you're on *my* half hour.

BRAD [*irritated*]. Are you cutting in on my call?

JAN. We made an agreement! You're on my time!

BRAD [*glancing at his watch*]. All right—so I overlapped by a few measly minutes. Does that give you a license to be rude?

JAN [*coldly*]. Have you anything else to say?

BRAD. Yes! Get off my back, lady! Stop living vicariously in what you think I do. [*He hangs up angrily, and so does she. As* JAN *bites her lip for control,* ALMA *calls to her.*]

ALMA [*off* U L, *cheerfully*]. New system working okay?

JAN [*getting up, more hurt than angry*]. About what you'd expect. [*She goes out* U L. *In the other apartment,* BRAD *throws down a sofa pillow angrily.*]

BRAD [*to himself*]. She needs a good lesson! She needs a—— [*He is interrupted by a brisk knock on his door. Calls* R, *sharply.*] Come in . . . the door's open.

[JONATHAN *comes in.*]

JONATHAN. Hi, Brad. You mad or something?

BRAD. I thought you'd be here earlier.

JONATHAN. Stopped off to see someone in the neighborhood. How's the show going? Got any more songs ready?

BRAD. Almost.

JONATHAN. Fine. Let's hear them.

BRAD. Not now, Jonathan. I've had a little irritation and it's thrown me off today. [*Rising.*] I'm going out.

JONATHAN. Just a minute, my boy! I'm putting two hundred thousand dollars into this show. We've got a theatre deadline to meet!

BRAD. You're hounding me!

JONATHAN. I don't know. Money seems to have lost its value these days. With two hundred thousand dollars, my grandfather cornered the wheat market and started a panic in Omaha! Today you can't even frighten songwriters with it.

BRAD. That's inflation for you. Pour yourself some coffee.

JONATHAN. Thanks. [*Helping himself.*] Trouble with you is, you're prejudiced against me because I'm part of a minority group.

BRAD [*puzzled*]. What minority group?

JONATHAN [*with mock bitterness*]. Millionaires. You outnumber us, but you'll never get us! We'll fight for our rights to the bitter end. And we've got the money to do it!

BRAD. Jonathan—are you actually bitter?

JONATHAN. You don't seem to realize what this show means to me! Look at us—you and me. We went through college together.

BRAD. I *worked* my way through.

JONATHAN. Yes, and now you've become an important songwriter. You've had a couple of big Broadway hits. You started out with nothing and you've really made something out of yourself.

BRAD [*bewildered*]. Well?

JONATHAN. Then take *me*. I started out in college with eight million dollars, and I've still got eight million dollars. I just can't seem to get ahead.

BRAD. Who's the girl?

JONATHAN. What girl?

BRAD [*smiling*]. Oh, come on now. You can't kid me. I've been through three marriages with you. You're like a fighter. You're only ambitious when you're getting ready to climb into the ring.

JONATHAN. Yeah. Well——There *is* a girl.

BRAD [*encouraging*]. Um?

JONATHAN [*intensely*]. Brad, she is the sweetest, she is the loveliest—she's the most talented person I've ever met.

BRAD. When's the—happy occasion?

JONATHAN. I don't know for sure. She claims she doesn't want to marry me. But that's what all my wives said at first. [*Picking up telephone.*] Mind if I call her?

BRAD. Go right ahead. What's her name?

JONATHAN. Jan.

BRAD [*innocently curious*]. Jan—who?

JONATHAN [*suddenly wary*]. I'm not telling you. I may be neurotic, but I'm not crazy. [*Putting down telephone.*] I'll call her later.

BRAD. No, no. Go ahead.

JONATHAN. Her line's always busy, anyway. She shares a party line with some nut.

BRAD. That's funny, I——[*Catching himself.*] Uh—what kind of a nut?

JONATHAN. Some guy with a phone fetish.

BRAD [*carefully*]. That's all you know about it?

JONATHAN [*amused*]. It's so bad she had to make a deal with him. They use the phone on alternate half-hours.

BRAD [*chuckling*]. Ridiculous! [*Casually.*] A pretty girl?

JONATHAN [*nodding*]. Wow——

BRAD. And you won't tell who she is?

JONATHAN. That's right. I found this gold mine. I'm not telling a claim-jumper like you how to get it!

BRAD. You sly dog, you.

JONATHAN. Brad, I only hope one day *you* find a girl like this. You ought to quit all this chasing around and get married.

BRAD. Why?

JONATHAN. Why? You're not getting any younger, fella. Oh, sure—it's fun, it's exciting—out dancing with a different doll every night. But there comes a time when a man wants to give up that kind of life.

BRAD. Why?

JONATHAN. Because he wants to create a stable, lasting relationship with one person. Brad, believe me—there's nothing so wonderful, so fulfilling, as coming home to the same woman every night.

BRAD. Why?

JONATHAN. Because! That's what it means to be adult. A wife, a family, a house. A mature man wants responsibilities.

BRAD. Why?

JONATHAN [*irked*]. Well, if you want to, you can find tricky arguments against anything. What have you got against marriage, anyway?

BRAD [*seriously*]. Jonathan . . . before a man gets married, he's—he's like a tree in the forest. He stands there independent—an entity unto himself. And then he's chopped down. His branches are cut off—and he's thrown into the river with the rest of the logs.

JONATHAN [*protesting*]. Now, Brad——

BRAD. Then this tree is taken to the mill—and when it comes out, it's no longer a tree. It's a vanity table, the breakfast nook, the baby crib.

JONATHAN [*horrified in spite of himself*]. No——

BRAD [*inflexibly*]. The newspaper that lines the family garbage can.

JONATHAN [*shaking finger in denial*]. If this girl weren't something *extra* special, then maybe I'd agree with you. But —but with Jan—[*With decision.*]—you look forward to having your branches cut off!

BRAD [*impressed*]. She *really* must be special.

JONATHAN. I have to be going. Listen—remember, I need those songs.

BRAD. I'll have 'em in your office on Monday.

JONATHAN [*going* R]. Good man!

[*As* JONATHAN *goes out* R, BRAD *looks after him thoughtfully for a minute. Then he picks up telephone and dials. The telephone rings in Jan's apartment.* JAN *hurries in and picks it up. She has changed to a semi-formal dress.*]

JAN. Hello?

BRAD [*heavy with contrition*]. Miss Morrow, this is Brad Allen. I've just gone through an agonizing reappraisal of our situation, and I'm not very proud of myself. I *have* been using the phone too much, and I've been extremely rude. I'd like to apologize, and I thought we could get together—have a cup of coffee, maybe—get acquainted. We might find we have a lot in common.

JAN [*unable to resist putting this in*]. I'm busy getting ready to go out, Mr. Allen. A party at the St. Regis. [*Coldly.*] We have nothing in common except this telephone. Not that meeting you mightn't prove amusing. But frankly, some jokes are just too obvious to be funny! [JAN *hangs up firmly, and goes back out.* BRAD *considers this momentary set-back, then looks in his book again, and dials another number.*]

[MARIE, *a tall, attractive, highly made-up "showgirl," wearing a dressing gown, steps on* D L *holding a telephone.*]

MARIE. Hello?

BRAD. Marie?

MARIE. Bradley, honey!

BRAD. Doing anything special before your last show goes on tonight?

MARIE. Love to see you—just so I get back to the Copa in time to get into my costume.

BRAD. I was thinking of one of those old-fashioned places where they still play Strauss waltzes while you have supper.

MARIE. I want to hear about your new show. But remember— I might have to run out on you to get back in time.

BRAD. That's what I figured—but we'll have a nice supper, anyway.

MARIE [*suddenly curious*]. Say, tell me—where do they still play Strauss waltzes? [*The lights are dimming.*]

BRAD. I was thinking—let's try the St. Regis. [*The lights are out. Immediately, however, almost on the words "St. Regis," the familiar strains of Strauss' "Blue Danube Waltz" are heard. The curtains are closed in front of the two apartments the moment the lights are out, and the remainder of this act takes place in front of the curtain. While this break is bridged by the music played at a good volume, it should be as short as possible.*]

[*The lights come up quickly in front of the curtain. Stagehands, who can be dressed as waiters, bring in two small tables, one from each side, and set them about one-third of the way in, each with two small chairs. MRS. WALTERS and JAN are strolling on L.*]

JAN [*a compliment*]. With your party taking up so much of the place, they keep setting out more tables.

MRS. WALTERS. You shouldn't leave so soon.

JAN [*smiling*]. I have some early appointments tomorrow. It's a marvelous party.

[TONY *is coming on* L.]

MRS. WALTERS. We'll have another—a housewarming—when you finish decorating.

TONY [*to* JAN]. I'm ready to go if you are.

JAN. Just about.

TONY. But I'd like *one* dance. I'm so desperate I'll even waltz.

JAN. Of course—but I haven't said good night to everyone.

TONY. Let's dance first. After the hours I've put in tonight, I should get something out of it.

MRS. WALTERS. Tony, couldn't you—just this once—come back and say good night to everyone?

TONY. Big deal.

MRS. WALTERS [*to* JAN]. If you can, try to drag this charming Phi Beta Kappa back to our table before he sees you home.

[*She goes out* L.]
TONY [*taking hold of* JAN'S *hand*]. Come on.

[BRAD *and* MARIE *are coming on* R.]

JAN [*confused, as he pulls her* R]. I thought you wanted to——
TONY. Look, Jan—the dancing's better on the terrace.
JAN [*being pulled along*]. Till we get in off that terrace, you
    better call me *Miss* Morrow. [BRAD *looks after them as they
    pass.*]
BRAD [*with satisfaction; he's made contact*]. *Miss* Morrow.
MARIE. What, honey?
BRAD [*indicating table*]. Sit right here.
MARIE [*doing so*]. You've been looking over this place like a
    private eye on television. [*Concerned.*] I'll have to be getting
    back to the Copa.
BRAD [*confidentially*]. Did you happen to notice that young
    man that just went by with the girl?
MARIE. Not especially.
BRAD. Dear—I'd *like* to use you in one of my shows, but it
    might look like favoritism. That young fellow represents a
    syndicate that invests heavily in musicals. [*With a gesture.*]
    Now if one of the *backers* wanted you to get a part——
MARIE [*doubtfully*]. That young guy?
BRAD [*concerned*]. If you could just get him down to see you
    at the Copa!

[JAN *and* TONY, *half-dancing and half-fencing, are coming
    back in* R.]

JAN. No more terrace.
TONY. Jan—there's something about a career girl——
JAN. Control yourself. Remember you're a Harvard man!
TONY. Not tonight. I'm on vacation.
JAN [*taking his hand from her shoulder*]. Stop it. You're only
    twenty-one.
TONY. I dig older women!

JAN. Tony, so help me—I'm going to tell your mother!

TONY. It's your word against mine!

JAN [*shoving him into chair at other table*]. Sit there while I say good night to the others—then you can see me to a taxi, and that's it.

TONY [*after her*]. Don't try to tell me what to do! [*But* JAN *stalks on off* L.]

MARIE [*doubtfully*]. I don't know. Maybe I'll just stay at the Copa.

BRAD [*confidentially*]. You could handle him. [*Forcefully.*] Marie—this could be your chance!

MARIE [*admiring*]. It's certainly nice of you—I mean, worrying about me.

BRAD [*with a shrug*]. That's show business. I'll just sit here with my thoughts.

MARIE [*getting up*]. I always wonder what you're really thinking. [*She crosses toward other table.*] Hello, there. Please— if I could trouble you? [BRAD *gets up, too, standing to the side.*]

TONY [*looking up, puzzled*]. Yes?

MARIE. If you're seeing girls to taxis—I have to get to the Copa. [*Takes slight pose.*] I'm a dancer.

TONY [*scrambling up*]. Hey——

MARIE. You're sure I'm not a bother? Maybe you're *with* someone.

TONY [*shrugging*]. A friend of my mother—and she can get her own taxi.

MARIE. Ever been to the Copa?

TONY [*as they're crossing* R]. Well, not recently——

[BRAD *waves appreciation at* MARIE *as she and* TONY *go by and out* R, *and then looks back* L *where* JAN *is coming in.*]

BRAD [*after seeing* JAN, *looking front, talking to himself*]. Jonathan wasn't kidding about *her!* Only how do I get on friendly terms——The minute I tell her my name, I'm dead! [JAN *has paused to look about, then sits, looking front.*]

JAN [*talking to herself*]. Now I've really hit bottom! It looks like I've been ditched by that miserable college boy.

BRAD [*having glanced at her again, looking front*]. Only—maybe I don't have to tell her. [*In a low voice, as though encouraging himself.*] Come on, boy—take a chance—play it by ear. [BRAD *is rising.*]

JAN [*having glanced at* BRAD, *looking front again*]. Now there's a fine-looking man——[*Steals a quick glance.*] I wonder if he's single. [BRAD *has started toward* JAN.]

BRAD [*calling to her, in a western drawl*]. 'Scuse me, ma'am.

JAN [*looking toward him again*]. Yes?

BRAD [*coming up to her*]. I reckon it got a mite close in here for your partner—and he left.

JAN. Oh—so he did.

BRAD. Shucks, ma'am—a place like this could about overpower anyone.

JAN [*flustered*]. This is very embarrassing. His mother is a client of mine.

BRAD. You a lawyer or something?

JAN. No. I'm an interior decorator.

BRAD. Y'are, huh? We don't get much call for that back home in Texas.

JAN. Texas.

BRAD. Just rolling range country. You could be in Australia.

JAN [*with growing approval*]. I expect you could, Mister—uh——

BRAD. Stetson, ma'am. Rex Stetson.

JAN. Well—I'd better be getting on home. [*The waiters take away the tables during this.*]

BRAD. It's mighty late for a young lady to be out alone.

JAN. I live nearby—a few blocks.

BRAD. It looked to me like that young fella was trying to force his attentions on ya.

JAN. Well——

BRAD. I can tell you we make short work of his kind back in Texas.

JAN [*admiring*]. I'll bet you do.

BRAD. I'd feel a lot better if you'd let me see you home.

JAN. That's very nice of you. [*As he takes her arm, the sound of traffic noises is heard, and they start walking slowly.* JAN *smiles nervously.*] Well, well——

BRAD. Yes? You started to say something?

JAN [*more nervous*]. I—uh——

BRAD [*encouraging*]. Now don't you be shy with me.

JAN. It's a lovely evening, isn't it?

BRAD. Oh, yes, ma'am——It sure is.

JAN [*blurting out*]. You married?

BRAD [*pausing, with a surprised intake of breath*]. Me?

JAN [*in an agony of embarrassment*]. Oh, I didn't mean——
[*Weakly.*] Just trying to make some casual conversation.

BRAD [*nervous himself now*]. Well—I—I—uh——

JAN [*earnestly*]. It's none of my business——

BRAD [*taking a breath and facing it*]. Ma'am—I'm not married.
[*To change subject, he points up and off.*] All those buildings filled up with people. It kind of scares a country boy like me.

JAN [*nodding* L]. Actually, I live in that building.

BRAD [*impressed*]. Imagine that!

JAN [*regarding him with considerable approval*]. You're certainly not like—well—you're——

BRAD. Go on——

JAN [*smiling*]. I'm trying to say, you're a welcome relief from the sort I see around here. Not just the little idiot at the St. Regis. I could tell you about another who's even worse!

BRAD [*with shock*]. No!

JAN. Yes!

BRAD [*regretfully*]. If this is where you live, this is where I leave you.

JAN [*eagerly*]. But—wouldn't you like to come in for some coffee?

BRAD. Oh, no, ma'am! I ain't used to these hours. Why, back home we'd just about be getting up now.

JAN [*hopefully*]. My apartment's right here.

BRAD. No, thank you. [*Starting* R.] But it's been a real pleasure, ma'am.

JAN [*after him*]. But then how will we——

BRAD [*pausing*]. Ma'am?

JAN [*stumped*]. Nothing.

BRAD [*starting R again*]. Then good night.

JAN [*calling after him*]. But, Mr. Stetson?

BRAD [*pausing again*]. Yes?

JAN [*getting idea*]. Seeing how you're all alone in New York
——Well, if there's anything you need and I can be of some
help, I'd like you to have my phone number——

BRAD [*repressing smile*]. That's very kind.

JAN [*speaking carefully so he'll remember*]. If you should want
to reach me, call PLaza two—two-seven-four-eight.

BRAD [*repeating*]. Two-two-seven——

JAN *and* BRAD [*together*]. four-eight.

BRAD [*starting R again*]. I'll remember that. [*He pauses at R to
look back at her. She's at L, looking across to him. BRAD turns
front, speaking to himself.*] I'd say five or six dates and she'll
be eating out of my hand!

JAN [*turning front and sighing*]. Oh—it's *so* nice——I've
finally met a man I can trust! [*They look back at each other
and wave.*]

BRAD. Good night.

JAN. Good night. [*Each steps off stage. The lights in front of
the curtain black out and then the houselights come up.*]

END OF ACT ONE

ACT TWO

AS THE HOUSELIGHTS DIM, *the familiar sound of* BRAD *working out a melody line at his piano is heard.*]

THE CURTAIN *rises to reveal the same set as in the previous act. Jan's living room is not occupied at the moment. In the other apartment* BRAD *is hard at work at his piano. He is trying to concentrate as he plays, and then writes notes on the music paper in front of him.* EILEEN, *wearing another high fashion dress, is also in Brad's apartment, delicately doing a bit of sofa pillow patting and ash tray positioning.*]

EILEEN [*pausing*]. Brad——[*As he continues working, she speaks louder.*] Brad!

BRAD [*arrested with his pencil in mid-air, without turning*]. Yes, Eileen.

EILEEN. You don't *mind*—my straightening up your apartment?

BRAD [*making an effort to be patient*]. The maid *already* straightened up, but no—I don't mind.

EILEEN [*earnestly*]. I wouldn't interfere with your work for anything.

BRAD [*as he goes back to it*]. If you really want to help, you could give the maid a hand with the mess I left in the kitchen. [EILEEN *has taken an absurd apron from her bag, which she is now tying in front of her fashionable dress.*]

EILEEN. I'll leave that to her. I mean, she knows where things go. [*He's too busy again to reply, and she has to demand his attention.*] Brad!

BRAD [*slamming down pencil, and turning*]. Now listen, Eileen——

EILEEN. I just wanted you to see the apron—[*Ready to cry.*]—which I bought especially.

BRAD [*briefly*]. It's lovely. But right now I have to finish this song.

42

EILEEN [*disapproving*]. You don't sound like the same old Brad.

BRAD. There comes a time when old Brad has to get his work done.

EILEEN [*a loud whisper*]. I won't say another word.

BRAD [*whispering back*]. You're *very* considerate. [*As* BRAD *resumes working,* EILEEN *looks about for her next good deed. She tiptoes to behind the loveseat and wheels out an upright vacuum cleaner. She considers the rug, decides it could use the cleaning, then switches on vacuum. It should be a very loud cleaner, and the sudden sound brings* BRAD *right up off the piano bench. He waves her to stop.*] Eileen! [*She turns it off.*]

EILEEN [*with shrug*]. I can't help it.

BRAD. Dear—the man's coming today for the last of these songs, and I'm not quite finished.

EILEEN. That's why I'm trying to help. [*There is a knock on the door.*]

BRAD. You see? [*Crossing to door.*] Here he is.

[BRAD *opens the door and* YVETTE *comes in carrying an attractively wrapped flower box.*]

YVETTE. *Cherie*——

EILEEN. Yes, I see.

BRAD [*startled*]. What are you doing here, Yvette?

YVETTE. I brought flowers.

BRAD [*irked*]. Why flowers?

YVETTE. It isn't like you not to call. I assumed you must be sick. [*Noting* EILEEN.] Is *this* your maid?

EILEEN [*snatching off apron*]. No.

BRAD [*with a shrug*]. *She* assumed I needed a spring cleaning.

YVETTE [*suspiciously*]. What *are* you up to, Brad?

BRAD. A crazy mood! [*Gestures toward piano.*] I thought I'd finish this work——it's almost done!

YVETTE. But what are you *really* up to?

BRAD [*insisting*]. But that's it!

EILEEN. I was leaving anyway.

YVETTE. I seem to've come at the wrong time. [*To* EILEEN.] If you're going uptown, we'll share a cab.

BRAD [*handing back flower box*]. It was a kind thought—but I don't think I'm sick.

YVETTE [*taking box*]. I'm not so sure.

EILEEN [*frankly*]. You don't seem normal to me.

BRAD [*shortly*]. Of course I am. [*Defensively.*] It's just the work. As soon as I'm myself again——[*To* EILEEN.] I'll be calling——[*To* YVETTE.] We'll have a ball. [*The girls exchange a raised-eyebrow look as they go out* R. BRAD *looks after them, faintly puzzled. Then he crosses to a small wall mirror, leans forward, sticks out his tongue and goes "Ahh." This doesn't convey anything, and he goes back to the piano. He mutters to himself.*] First, finish the work. Second, settle with Jan Morrow——[*With relish.*] *Then* get back to normal. [BRAD *barely re-starts with the piano when he is bothered by a thought which brings him to a stop. He calls out to kitchen.*] Bessie——Hey, Bess——

BESSIE [*from kitchen*]. Yes, Mr. Allen.

BRAD [*as though it's almost too silly to voice*]. Bessie—wouldn't you say that I'm perfectly normal?

BESSIE [*from kitchen*]. No, sir.

BRAD [*a bit put out, but managing a smile*]. Well——Do I strike you as more abnormal—*recently?*

BESSIE [*from kitchen*]. Yes, sir.

BRAD [*getting up from piano, demanding*]. Bessie—what makes you say a thing like that?

[BESSIE, *a pleasant woman wearing a maid uniform, comes in from the kitchen holding a big cowboy hat, a lariat, and any other obvious "western" paraphernalia.*]

BESSIE. *This* makes me say a thing like that——You bought yourself a cowboy outfit.

BRAD. Oh——yes.

BESSIE. You've got everything but a horse and saddle. [*Putting things down.*] I'm finished for the day.

BRAD. Next Friday, as usual?

BESSIE [*nodding*]. On my way out, I'll put a new name slip
by your bell. I noticed when I was coming in. I don't know
how it could've been lost.

BRAD. That's all right—never mind.

BESSIE. But suppose someone came—they couldn't find your
name on the bell.

BRAD. It's—well—intentional. I'll put in a new name slip later.

BESSIE [*looking at him with wonder*]. I can't even *guess* what
you have in mind.

BRAD [*conceding*]. It's getting pretty complicated.

BESSIE [*going*]. Well—see you Friday—pardner. [BRAD *smiles
after her as she goes out* R, *then sits down and goes back to
work. He only touches a few notes and then starts working
directly on the music paper.*]

[*In Jan's apartment,* PIEROT *comes out of the kitchen and
crosses to the desk.*]

PIEROT [*calling back*]. Jan—did you leave the color charts on
your desk? Jan? [*But there is no answer.* PIEROT *shakes his
head and starts looking himself. He mutters:*] No help at all.

[*Two well-dressed women,* MRS. FROST *and* MRS. AMES, *come in
from the kitchen.*]

MRS. FROST [*is saying*]. It's a pity to leave, but we can just
make the next train for Scarsdale.

MRS. AMES [*to* PIEROT]. Your associate makes you do all the
work.

PIEROT [*explaining*]. She puts in such long hours, she gets a
little absent-minded, sometimes.

[JAN *is coming in* U L.]

JAN [*concerned*]. You're not going already?

MRS. AMES. It was nice to have this tea, and the—the preliminary discussion.

JAN [*contrite*]. I'll be much better prepared at our next meeting.

PIEROT. Jan—where are the color comparison charts?

JAN. They should be——[*Shakes head.*] I just can't remember.

MRS. FROST. They're not important. We'll see them next time.

MRS. AMES. Mrs. Walters certainly gives you a fine recommendation!

MRS. FROST. I think I saw you with her son Tony—at the St. Regis.

JAN. Well—yes.

MRS. FROST. Such a versatile boy.

JAN [*pleasantly*]. Oh, he's versatile!

MRS. AMES. I understand his big interest now is—show business.

MRS. FROST. We'll be in touch.

PIEROT [*opening door for them*]. I'm going, too. Let me put you in a taxi. [*They go on out* L *and* PIEROT *turns back to* JAN.] Jan—what's the matter?

JAN. Nothing.

PIEROT. For a well-organized, full-time career girl, you sure day-dreamed through that conference.

JAN [*softly*]. I'm sorry.

PIEROT. Probably no harm done. [*Going.*] But what were you thinking about? [*She gives him a small smile and a helpless shrug. He shakes his head and goes out* L. JAN *takes a breath, then snaps her fingers several times in front of her face. She's not snapped out of anything.*]

JAN [*to herself, exasperated*]. That's right! What am I thinking about?

[ALMA *comes in from kitchen with tray and begins picking up used ash trays as she speaks.*]

ALMA. Him. That's who you're thinking about. The cowboy.

JAN. Well, at least he respected me. Didn't even try to kiss me.

ALMA. Hmm.

JAN. Or maybe I just didn't appeal to him.

ALMA. Did he write down your telephone number?

JAN. Well—no.

ALMA. Where's he staying?

JAN [*ruefully*]. I didn't think to ask.

ALMA. Hmm. [*Goes out with ash trays.* JAN *sits down unhappily. Meanwhile,* BRAD *has written something with a flourish on his music paper and gets up.*]

BRAD [*delighted*]. The finale—finished! It's done! [*Turning toward his telephone, with relish.*] And now for Miss Morrow. [*He dials the telephone, then as he waits he reaches down, picks up his cowboy hat and puts it on. The telephone rings in Jan's apartment, and she jumps. With an effort she composes herself and picks up the telephone.*]

JAN. Hello.

BRAD [*his Texas drawl*]. Uh, ma'am . . . this is Rex Stetson.

JAN [*relieved and happy as she recognizes his voice, but keeping herself in check*]. Oh! Hello!

BRAD. I hope I didn't disturb you.

JAN. Disturb? *You?* [*Managing a more moderate tone.*] No, not at all.

BRAD. I was just sittin' here thinkin' about your generous offer and all—to call you in case there was anythin' I needed.

JAN. Um-hm?

BRAD. I need to go out for dinner tomorrow night and I sure would enjoy seein' a friendly face across the table. 'Course, if you're gonna be busy tomorrow night——

JAN [*quickly*]. Oh, no! I always keep tomorrow night open! I mean—I hadn't—I hadn't planned a thing! Oh, I'd *love* to have dinner with you. [BRAD *smiles and reaches out to jiggle the receiver.* JAN *is concerned.*] Hello—what is it?

BRAD [*removing his hat, speaking in his natural voice*]. Hello, hello, hello! Is anybody on this line?

JAN [*sharply*]. Yes, I'm on the line! Would you please get off it?

BRAD. Why?

JAN [*urgently*]. *Please!*

BRAD. Oh, all right—but you're on *my* half hour!

JAN. Rex! Rex, are you there?

BRAD [*back in drawl*]. Uh, yes, ma'am. Who was that?

JAN. That was my party line! A horrible little man!

BRAD. He sure isn't very well-mannered.

JAN. Mannered? He isn't even worth talking about! Now. [*Sighs.*] What were you saying?

BRAD. I've never been much on makin' fancy speeches, but I get a nice, warm feeling bein' near you, ma'am. It's like—like bein' 'round a pot-bellied stove on a frosty mornin'.

JAN [*sighing*]. Oh, Rex! What a *lovely* thing to say!

BRAD. I don't want to be forward, ma'am, but I'm so anxious to see you. Could we move up our dinner engagement to *this* evening?

JAN. That would be——[*Remembers.*] Oh, I forgot—— [*Miserable.*] I already have a date for tonight.

BRAD. Who with?

JAN. A client. You don't know him. Jonathan Forbes.

BRAD. 'Course you ain't the kind of gal who'd break a date.

JAN. No, I'm not.

BRAD. And I ain't the kind of guy who'd ask you to.

JAN. I know you're not.

BRAD. I'll pick you up in an hour.

JAN. I'll be ready. [*He hangs up, and then she does. To herself, softly.*] Wow! [*Dreamily.*] Like a pot-bellied stove on a frosty morning! [*Hugs herself.*] Gosh!

BRAD [*smugly*]. Everything right on schedule! [BRAD, *well satisfied with himself, gets up and goes out into the other room, unbuttoning his shirt to change it, as he goes. Meanwhile* JAN *has sighed again, and gets up from her chair with a look of supreme happiness on her face.*]

[ALMA *is coming in from the kitchen.*]

ALMA. He *must* be pretty special.

JAN [*not quite focusing*]. What do you mean?

ALMA. For you to break a date for him.

JAN [*pained*]. The extension? [ALMA *nods, but* JAN *would rather discuss than be angry.*] Well, he *is* special.

ALMA. Could you spare a few details?

JAN [*with enthusiasm*]. He's—he's tall, handsome, intelligent. And he comes from rolling range country in Texas—[*Making point.*]—which is a lot like Australia.

ALMA [*smiling*]. Then don't just stand there! Get yourself up so pretty you'll rock him right off his range.

JAN. I'd like to——[*Hesitating.*] Of course I don't really know much about him.

ALMA. You know he's a change from the men you've been complaining about around here.

JAN [*nodding*]. The first thing I noticed—he's sincere, and so straight-from-the-shoulder.

ALMA. And handsome and intelligent. [*Frankly.*] An opportunity like that from Texas doesn't come along every day.

JAN [*her hesitation lingering*]. Still—we didn't actually get to talk a lot.

ALMA. My father used to say—only takes *one* sip of wine to tell if it's a good bottle.

JAN [*coming to a decision*]. You're right. This *is* a good bottle!

ALMA. He sounded good to me. [*Faintly puzzled.*] While I was listening—there was something about his voice——[*Shakes her head.*] But I *couldn't* know him. I don't know *anyone* from Texas.

JAN. I'm just glad I had the good luck to meet him. [*A wry confession.*] I have a feeling this is going to matter even more than I thought.

ALMA [*impressed*]. First time I've heard *you* talk this way. [*There is a knock on the door.*]

JAN [*as she crosses to door, smiling*]. First time there's been someone worth talking about. [*She opens door, greeting the caller in a pleasant but casual tone.*] Oh, hello, Jonathan.

[JONATHAN *strides in, looking dissatisfied.*]

JONATHAN. What do you mean—"Oh, hello, Jonathan."

JAN. You're *hours* too early. [*Uneasily.*] I was going to phone **you.**

JONATHAN. Just dropped in for a moment now. I happened to be in the neighborhood, anyway, because I have to see——— [*Stops himself. Suspiciously.*] *Why* were you going to phone?

JAN [*embarrassed*]. It's about tonight.

ALMA [*fleeing out to kitchen*]. I've some clearing up.

JONATHAN. What about tonight?

JAN. If you wouldn't mind, I—I'd———

JONATHAN [*accusing*]. You're planning to break our date——— yes?

JAN [*with a sigh*]. Yes.

JONATHAN [*horrified*]. You admit it!

JAN [*contrite*]. I *hate* doing a thing like this, but———

JONATHAN [*cutting in*]. *Why* are you breaking our date? Now tell the truth! 'Cause you've got another date, huh? Go ahead —tell me! You're going out with someone else—right?

JAN. Right.

JONATHAN [*crushed*]. That's a *terribly* cruel thing to say! Who is he? What's his name?

JAN. Rex Stetson.

JONATHAN. Do I know him?

JAN. No. He's visiting here from Texas.

JONATHAN. Texas?

JAN. Um-hm.

JONATHAN. Jan—how could you? How could you fall in love with a tourist?

JAN [*smiling and shrugging*]. I don't know. I just did.

JONATHAN [*the district attorney*]. You admit that, too! You just said it! You love him!

JAN [*surprised at herself*]. I did, didn't I? [*Amused at herself.*] But it's a bit soon, don't you think?

JONATHAN [*sinking into chair*]. As many times as I'll be married, I'll never understand women! [*Despairing.*] What a blow to my psyche—to be rejected for a cowboy!

JAN. He's not a cowboy.

JONATHAN. All right—an oil man! Jan, if you marry him, you'll have to live out there!

JAN. I guess I would.

JONATHAN [*getting up*]. Jan, I want you to look at something. [*He gestures toward her window.*] New York! People— jostling, shoving, struggling, milling, fighting for their lives! And you're part of it!

JAN. Well?

JONATHAN. In Texas there's nothing but—a bunch of prairie dogs and stuff. And even the air out there! There's *nothing* in it but air. In New York you've got air you can sink your teeth into. [*Inhaling with relish.*] It has character!

JAN. But, Jonathan——

JONATHAN. Don't you see—you *can't* live in Texas.

JAN. This is silly. Besides—we're a *long* way from starting any talk about marriage.

JONATHAN. Yeh—but that look in your eye! I've been married often enough to know when a girl's willing to talk about it!

JAN. Do I look willing?

JONATHAN. You look absolutely disgusting!

JAN [*kissing him on his cheek*]. Thank you.

JONATHAN [*apologizing*]. I'm sorry. You know me. I say an awful lot of things I don't mean. [*Glancing at watch, embarrassed.*] I'm late for an appointment.

JAN [*earnestly*]. I wish you good luck with everything, Jonathan—that show you're producing, your next wife——

JONATHAN [*pausing at door*]. I just hope you'll be happy, Jan —I mean, without me! [*Bravely.*] If it's Rex Stetson you want, I hope it's Rex Stetson you get! [JONATHAN *goes out* L. JAN *looks after him for a moment, then inhales deeply and exhales.*]

JAN [*to herself*]. It's more important for the *man* to have character.

[*As* JAN *is crossing to glance out her window,* BRAD *is coming back into the other apartment. He's changed to a white shirt and he's put on a tie.*]

BRAD [*crossing to telephone and starting to dial; with pleasant anticipation and a wicked smile*]. Now for the *next* step—— [*The telephone starts ringing in Jan's apartment.*]

JAN [*crossing quickly from window*]. Maybe it's——[*Picking up the telephone.*] Hello?

BRAD [*briskly*]. Miss Morrow—this is Brad Allen. Hello? Hello?

JAN [*briefly*]. Yes?

BRAD. When I picked up the phone a while ago—well, I couldn't help overhearing part of your conversation.

JAN. I'm sure you couldn't.

BRAD. Sharing a phone together, I feel a certain responsibility for you. Now look—I've been thinking about this, and I want you to take my advice. *Don't* go out with that man tonight. He's a phony. Of course it's none of my business——

JAN. That's right, Mr. Allen! It is none of your business.

BRAD. Okay. Only don't let that yokel art fool you. This ranch-hand-Romeo is just trying to win your confidence—lull you into a false sense of security.

JAN [*sharply*]. Don't judge other people by yourself.

BRAD. All right—if you won't take a friendly warning. But I can tell you exactly what he'll do!

JAN. You could no more understand a fine man like that than you could——

BRAD [*suppressing his amusement as he cuts in*]. Wait and see. I can predict the whole thing. He'll find some transparent excuse to have you stop up for a moment at wherever it is he's staying. And *then*, Miss Morrow, you'll be fighting off more passes than——

JAN [*furious*]. Good night, Mister Allen. [*She slams down the receiver.*] Ohh! [BRAD, *delighted, hangs up, then picks up the telephone and starts dialing again.* JAN *calls, meanwhile, toward kitchen.*] Alma—I hope you heard that!

ALMA [*from kitchen, indignant*]. I certainly did! And I'm just as mad as you are. [*The telephone rings again, and* JAN *snatches it up.*]

JAN [*her anger still showing*]. Yes?

BRAD [*back into his Texas drawl*]. Ma'am? Had a mite of trouble reachin' you. That busy signal kept a-goin' like a bullfrog on a summer night.

JAN. It was——[*Catching herself, and speaking calmly.*] It was that man who cut in on us before—only this time he wasn't just stupid, he was vicious.

BRAD [*earnestly*]. Maybe you should report him to the telephone company.

JAN [*embarrassed*]. I'd rather not talk about it.

BRAD. Ma'am, you've done a terrible thing to me. That's what I called to tell you.

JAN [*concerned*]. Oh?

BRAD. You've made me glad I ain't in Texas.

JAN [*with relief*]. Have I?

BRAD. Every time I look at you I say to myself, "We got all kinds of natural resources back home, but we ain't got nothin' like that!"

JAN [*laughing*]. Oh, Rex!

BRAD. I kinda hated New York when I first came here. All those people seemed so distant and all. Don't seem that way now.

JAN. Well, that's good. You'll find most people are willing to meet you halfway—if you'll let them.

BRAD [*blandly*]. Now that brings me to the other reason for my call.

JAN [*a bit wary in spite of herself*]. The other reason?

BRAD. You see, I'm staying just a few doors from where you live. A friend is letting me use his apartment. It's in the new corner building at Fifth.

JAN [*increasingly wary*]. Then you don't have to come very far to pick me up.

BRAD. That's just it, ma'am. I'd like you to stop up here——

JAN [*dismayed*]. You would?

BRAD. For just a moment——[*Friendly concern.*] I don't think you can see Central Park from your place—but what a view from this apartment!

JAN [*trying to put this off casually*]. Rex—I've *seen* Central Park.

BRAD. But not from here! I'll be waiting for you down in front. [*With this,* BRAD *hangs up and regards the telephone with amusement.*]

JAN [*anxiously*]. No, wait. Rex? [*Realizing he's hung up, she does the same. Disappointed.*] Oh, no! [BRAD *starts gathering his music together into a folder.*]

ALMA [*from kitchen*]. Maybe you better call him back and say——

JAN [*calling to* ALMA]. I don't have his number.

[ALMA *has come to kitchen door* U L.]

ALMA. Then what are you going to do?

JAN. Give my hair a brush and go meet him on the corner.

ALMA [*considering*]. I guess you're strong enough to defend yourself.

JAN. I've managed so far. [*Going out* U L, *past* ALMA.] Maybe it isn't such a bad idea to find out if Mr. Stetson is really as fine as I think he is. [JAN *has gone out* U L *and* ALMA *is following.*]

ALMA. Sure—but maybe you shouldn't pretty yourself up too much. [*There is a knock on Brad's door.*]

BRAD [*calling*]. Who is it?

JONATHAN [*off* R]. Jonathan——

BRAD [*shouting back as he ducks the cowboy things behind love seat*]. You were supposed to be here a long time ago. I didn't think you were coming.

JONATHAN. I can't resist hearing your latest excuse for not finishing the music. [*Banging on door.*] Come on——Open up.

BRAD [*looking at his watch*]. Just a moment——[*Taking telephone off cradle.*] I'm on the phone. [*Setting down telephone, he steps over to the door and opens it.*]

[JONATHAN *comes in* R.]

JONATHAN [*as he comes in*]. You don't seem very glad to see me.

BRAD. I *finished* the music. It's there on the piano—solid gold hit songs! Why don't you take them right home and look them over? Then we can discuss them later. [*The rush act.*] See you later, Jonathan.

JONATHAN. Finished! [*Sitting on piano bench and opening up the folder.*] This is an unexpected pleasure. I'll look them over here.

BRAD. Right now? [JONATHAN, *busy with music, nods.*] Excuse me. The phone. [*Picks up telephone and pretends to continue a conversation.*] Fred, you've *gotta* come over here fast and help me out! Fred, I'll make you a deal—if you'll get right over here and take this girl off my hands, I'll—Fred? Fred? [*Putting telephone back.*] He hung up.

JONATHAN. Fred who?

BRAD [*considering him*]. Say—it's a break you dropped in just now.

JONATHAN [*suspiciously*]. Why?

BRAD. There's somebody coming I want you to meet.

JONATHAN. I have my own problems. Remember that gal I told you about—Jan?

BRAD. Who?

JONATHAN. Jan. The one with the party line with the nut?

BRAD. Ohh, yeah. Well, what about her?

JONATHAN. She meets this stupid cowboy from Texas—of all places—and she falls for him!

BRAD. How do you know?

JONATHAN. She told me so. But don't worry—I'll break it up.

BRAD. You will?

JONATHAN. Yeah!

BRAD. How?

JONATHAN. Leave it to me. I don't know how fast he moves, but it takes an early bird to get the best of a worm like me.

[*In the other apartment* JAN *comes in from the door* U L, *picks up her gloves and purse, and goes out* L.]

BRAD [*admiring*]. No one puts anything over on you. [*With relief.*] And am I glad you're here! [*Gestures toward telephone.*] I mean, after the way Fred acted.

JONATHAN. I don't understand.

BRAD. Because of this girl I want you to meet.

JONATHAN. Who is it?

BRAD. A friend of the family. She's visiting.

JONATHAN. Oh.

BRAD. Wonderful girl.

JONATHAN. Uh-huh.

BRAD. But I'm stuck with more work tonight—and she'll be here any minute. [*As though suddenly getting an idea.*] Say, why don't *you* take her over for the evening?

JONATHAN. Me?

BRAD. Yes—take her dancing maybe. She's dying to learn how to dance.

JONATHAN. She doesn't know how to dance?

BRAD. Well, naturally, she doesn't get out of the house very often.

JONATHAN. What do you mean, "naturally"?

BRAD. Jonathan, believe me, you and Moose—I mean Miss Taggett—will get along——

JONATHAN. Moose!

BRAD. All right—so a girl picks up a nickname! You know how cruel kids can be—especially to someone who's a little—different.

JONATHAN. Just a minute! How different?

BRAD. Well, just—different.

JONATHAN. I see.

BRAD. *Please* stay, Jonathan. If you go right now, you'll miss her.

JONATHAN. Sorry, pal. I have to run. [*Explaining.*] I told you —I have to break up this silly business with the cowboy.

BRAD. I know——[*Pretending artfulness.*] But you can spare a few minutes. Have a cup of coffee.

JONATHAN. Oh, no, you don't! I won't stop running till I'm four blocks from here!

BRAD. Wait——

JONATHAN [*taking folder*]. I just came for the music. [*Crossing to door.*] The moose is all yours! [*With a superior smile as he goes out.*] Happy hunting! [JONATHAN *closes door,*

*and if desired there can be the brief sound here of someone
running away.* BRAD'S *anxious expression gives way to a
smile.*]

BRAD. Yes, indeedy! [BRAD *brings out the cowboy things again
and puts them where they'll be seen. Then he puts on his
suit coat, crosses to the door* R, *glances out first, and then
goes out.*]

[*Meanwhile,* D L, *a man wearing a trench coat comes in carrying
a telephone.*]

GRAHAM [*calling back to someone off* L]. You're sure its Jonathan Forbes? And he wants to talk to me again? [*Apparently
he receives affirmative answers.*] Okay—put him right on.
[*Into telephone.*] Hello . . . Mr. Forbes? [*A bit concerned.*] Mr. Forbes, is anything the matter?

[JONATHAN *comes on* D R *holding a telephone. He is breathing
heavily.*]

JONATHAN [*catching his breath*]. No, nothing's the matter.
I was running and then I stopped at this phone booth be-
cause I want you to get started right away——[*Hesitates.*]
This *is* the detective agency?

GRAHAM. Oh, yes, Mr. Forbes. [*Confidentially.*] You're on the
run?

JONATHAN. No, no—I was dodging a moose. The reason I
called——

GRAHAM [*bewildered*]. A *moose?*

JONATHAN. Forget the moose! I want you to get started on
Rex Stetson.

GRAHAM [*all business*]. Gotcha—the moose is out! We start
on Stetson!

JONATHAN. All I know is that his name is Rex Stetson and he's
from Texas! I want all the information you can get on him.

GRAHAM [*hesitating*]. Could you give us a *little* more to go on?

JONATHAN. Look—you've helped me get divorced three times.

Now let's see if you can get me married once.

GRAHAM [*his bewilderment growing*]. Get you married?

JONATHAN [*impatiently*]. I guess I'll have to come over and spell it out for you.

GRAHAM. Please.

JONATHAN. Be there in a few minutes. Better alert your whole staff. Get more people if you need them. If you've got a panic button, *push it!* [JONATHAN *looks furtively right and left, then hurries out* R. GRAHAM *expels a held breath and blinks his eyes as he goes off* L.]

[*There's a knock on the door of Brad's apartment, and then the door is opened from the outside.* JAN, *stony-faced, comes in, followed by* BRAD, *who is blandly cheerful.*]

BRAD. Well, ma'am, this is it.

JAN. This is what?

BRAD. Where I'm staying. [*Looking around.*] I see we have the place to ourselves.

JAN. I see.

BRAD. Aren't these New York apartments cozy little things?

JAN. Your friend who has this apartment——Do you expect him back soon?

BRAD. Well—no.

JAN [*her disillusion growing as she echoes his answer*]. No——— [*Takes a breath.*] When I was coming, I saw someone running in the other direction. That couldn't have been your friend?

BRAD [*innocently*]. I wouldn't think so. Why would he be clearing out like that?

JAN [*coldly*]. You tell me.

BRAD. Seems like they're *all* in a hurry here.

JAN [*with faint sarcasm*]. But not you?

BRAD [*sitting on love seat*]. Come on over here. [*There are some coffee things on a small coffee table in front of love seat, and* BRAD *starts arranging some sugar cubes.*]

JAN. Why? [*Curious at his actions.*] Is this some kind of game?

BRAD [*busy with arrangement*]. I want to show you something.

JAN [*sitting nervously on the edge of the love seat as far as she can get from him, intensely suspicious*]. Such as what?

BRAD [*indicating arrangement*]. Now—over here is the ranch house. And this cup over here—that's the corral. That's where I keep my ponies.

JAN [*starting to get up*]. It must be a very nice ranch.

BRAD [*putting a restraining hand on her shoulder*]. Wait—that isn't all.

JAN [*swallowing*]. Oh?

BRAD [*pulling a small pillow from in back of the tense JAN*]. If you don't mind—thank you. [*He sets it on the table.*] You see, over here behind the ranch house—this mountain. [*Indicating pillow.*] 'Taint a very big mountain, but it's ours. [*Getting up.*] Well, that gives you a rough idea.

JAN [*cautiously*]. And that's it?

BRAD. Yes, ma'am.

JAN [*beginning to relax*]. You just wanted to show me your place. [*Managing a smile.*] Imagine—your own mountain!

BRAD. Now for the real reason I asked you up. [*Standing by his window.*] Please—come here.

JAN [*her nervousness coming back*]. The real reason——

BRAD [*as she crosses to him, looking out*]. Now—ain't that a pretty view of Central Park?

JAN [*apprehensively*]. Yes.

BRAD. Mighty romantic, ain't it? [*She tenses as he takes her arm. Casually, leading her.*] Well—let's go.

JAN. Go?

BRAD. Sure. [*Blandly.*] You've *seen* the view.

JAN [*her faith in mankind being restored; half to herself*]. That's really why you asked me up.

BRAD [*as though puzzled*]. What'd you think?

JAN [*embarrassed*]. Uh—well, I thought——

BRAD. Thought what, ma'am?

JAN. Well, I—I thought you——[*With an embarrassed laugh.*] Give some men half a chance, and right away they're trying to kiss you.

BRAD. And you thought I——[*Hurt.*] Oh—ma'am!

JAN. I'm sorry, Rex.

BRAD [*being big about it*]. Quite all right.

JAN [*contrite*]. I should have *known* you're not like the others. Will you forgive me?

BRAD. 'Course, ma'am. Can't blame you. Livin' in bear country's bound to make you wonder about strange caves.

JAN [*glowing as she considers* BRAD]. It's wonderful to be able to feel *sure* about someone.

BRAD. I noticed they've got some horse-drawn hansom cabs goin' through the park. I thought we'd go for a drive—back-home style.

JAN. I'd *love* to!

BRAD [*as they cross*]. Know somethin'? Whenever I wanta feel close to home, the only thing that helps is gettin' behind a hoss. [*He opens the door* R.]

JAN. I hope you won't mind my saying this—but there's something so *wholesome* about a man who loves animals. [*She smiles and goes out* R. BRAD'S *eyes widen for an instant at her comment, and he smothers a smile. The lights are dimming.*]

BRAD [*following her out*]. I'll shore enjoy takin' you for a ride, ma'am. [*The lights are out. In the darkness, traffic sounds are heard, and with them the clop-clop-clop of a horse drawing a carriage. The horse whinnies, and then the sound starts fading off into the distance.*]

[*A spot of light comes up at* D R, *revealing* JONATHAN *standing with his arms folded.* GRAHAM, *in his trench coat and carrying a brief case, is coming up to him.*]

JONATHAN. Have you made *any* progress?

GRAHAM [*hedging*]. We're going all out!

JONATHAN. From the way the girl sounds, so is Rex Stetson.

GRAHAM [*confidently*]. Won't be long before we have more on him. I have men digging for information about Rex Stetson all over Texas.

JONATHAN. That's fine, but meanwhile——

GRAHAM [*cutting in*]. Meanwhile he's being followed on every date. They've had four so far. [*Hesitating.*] Uh—Mr. Forbes?

JONATHAN [*grimly*]. Give me the facts.

GRAHAM. It seems to be a very platonic relationship.

JONATHAN [*to himself, worried*]. So he wants to marry her, too!

GRAHAM [*opening his brief case*]. One of my operatives carries a secret camera. He got a very clear picture of Rex Stetson. [*Handing him photograph.*] Here's an enlargement.

JONATHAN [*taking photo*]. Let me look at that lummox from——[*Stunned.*] This isn't Rex Stetson!

GRAHAM. He's the one dating Jan Morrow.

JONATHAN. I can't believe it! This man—he's my best friend!

GRAHAM [*unimpressed*]. Yep.

JONATHAN. This is a terrible shock! What do you mean— "yep"?

GRAHAM. I mean your best friend, they're *usually* the one.

JONATHAN [*furious*]. I don't care what it costs, we've got to stop him. And *I* want to handle the finish!

GRAHAM. Finish?

JONATHAN. As soon as you get them spotted out together, let me know where they are and I'll come right over. [*They start off* R *together.*] If you need any more help for this, get those men back from Texas. [*As they go out* R, *a telephone starts ringing.*]

[*At this point, either the light comes up generally in the two apartments, or if preferred, spotlights can pick out the "telephone" area in both apartments. In either case,* BRAD *is revealed at the telephone in his apartment and* JAN *is revealed picking up the telephone in her apartment. Both are dressed to go out.* NOTE: *This costume change can be handled quickly by adding to, or substituting something for, what they were wearing before.*]

JAN [*into telephone*]. Hello. Who is it?

BRAD. Miss Morrow? Brad Allen.

JAN. Oh, look—I'm in a hurry, Mr. Allen, so if you don't mind——

BRAD. Of course, but before I hang up, just admit I was right.

JAN. About what?

BRAD. Your western gentleman. I've been meaning to call you about this. He turned out to be a prairie wolf, didn't he?

JAN. Mr. Allen, this may come as a shock, but there are some men whose minds are *not* on the same level as yours!

BRAD. Oh, come on! You mean he didn't try to get you up to see the view from his place or something like that?

JAN [*briskly*]. Yes, he had me up to the place where he's staying.

BRAD. Ah-ha!

JAN. Then he *showed* me the view, and then we left.

BRAD. And nothing else?

JAN. Nothing.

BRAD. Hm. That's even worse than I thought.

JAN. Worse? What do you mean—worse?

BRAD. Well—either you're not telling the truth, or——

JAN. Or what?

BRAD. Or maybe you just don't appeal to him that way.

JAN. What makes you say——

BRAD. Well, some men never really grow up. They stay tied to their mother's apron strings. Oh, they're *perfect* gentlemen, all right, but they're still so devoted to their mothers—they collect cooking recipes.

JAN. You *couldn't* be more wrong. [*Emphatically.*] I can't imagine anyone more grown-up, more adult, more——

BRAD. But he's never tried to kiss you.

JAN. That doesn't prove anything. It just happens we're going out tonight, and—and—well, it's none of your business.

BRAD [*smiling*]. Have a nice time, Miss Morrow.

JAN. No need for you to worry, Mr. Allen. [*As they hang up, the light on them goes out, and the curtains are closing in front of the two apartments.*]

[*A spot comes up at* L. GRAHAM *is hurrying across the stage toward the light.*]

GRAHAM [*as he crosses*]. Mr. Forbes—Mr. Forbes!

[JONATHAN *is coming in from the other direction.*]

JONATHAN. Yes—what is it? [*They meet at the spot of light.*]
GRAHAM. We've got them located for you.
JONATHAN. Where?
GRAHAM. One of my men just phoned to say they went into a little club known as the Hidden Door.
JONATHAN. The Hidden Door?
GRAHAM. A little supper club—has a girl singer. The music is strictly jazz.
JONATHAN [*worried*]. I hope they'll stay put till I get there. I can't imagine Jan in a jazz joint!
GRAHAM. My man thinks they'll stay. He said that Miss Morrow and—and your friend seem to be having a good time.
JONATHAN [*bitterly*]. My friend! Come on——[*As they start off* R.] I should've listened to my psychiatrist. He told me never to trust anyone but him! [*Immediately some good jazz music is heard, with a girl singing.* NOTE: *This can be on a record entirely, or the record can be instrumental with the girl who plays the role of "singer" singing along with the music from offstage. Three small tables are brought in from* R *and set near each other, each with two chairs.*]

[*As the lights come up on the area before the curtain,* BRAD *and* JAN *are revealed sitting at the table nearest* C. *Another couple is sitting at the next table, and the third table is empty.* NOTE: *If desired, more tables and more extras may be used here. The atmosphere is festive, and some colored light effects may be used. The song is concluding, and as it does,* BRAD *and* JAN *and the other couple applaud, an applause that should be enhanced from offstage to suggest more of a crowd. This can also be helped by playing a "crowd noise" sound effect at a low level.*]

JAN [*happy*]. Oh, this is fun. Like the song?
BRAD. Loved it! Mmm!

[*A* GIRL *wearing a very colorful dress is coming on from the direction of the music,* L.]

GIRL [*speaking generally*]. That's all for this session. The next starts at eleven. In the meantime, we'll have dance music—— [*She gestures back, and some dance music begins being played quietly* (*records*). *The girl notices* BRAD *and starts toward them.*]

BRAD [*feeling his pockets*]. I seem to be out of cigarettes. Maybe I'd better——

GIRL [*calling to him*]. Hello, there.

BRAD [*guarded*]. Oh, hello. We certainly enjoyed your singing.

GIRL [*patting his shoulder as she passes*]. When are you going to let me introduce one of your songs? [*She smiles and goes on.*]

JAN [*puzzled*]. One of your songs?

BRAD. Probably means a song from out West.

JAN. But——

BRAD. I'm afraid my hayseeds are that obvious.

[*Another couple is coming in from* L. *It's* TONY *and* MARIE.]

JAN. But she said——[*Notices* TONY *and* MARIE, *and puts hand up, shading her brow.*] Oh, dear! There's someone I'd just as soon avoid.

BRAD [*noticing, then ducking in the same way*]. Let's both avoid them. [TONY *and* MARIE *pass, arm in arm, giggling, and sit at the far table.*]

JAN [*laughing as she takes her hand away*]. I'm having such a wonderful time—I just don't want to bother with anyone else in the world.

BRAD [*laughing with her*]. Neither do I! [*Then calculating.*] You know, there's someone back home who's always saying the same thing you just said—about not bothering with anyone else.

JAN. Oh, who's that?

BRAD [*casually*]. My mother.

JAN. Your——[*Registering on this, but keeping casual.*] I see. Your mother.

BRAD. I'll want to tell her about the work you do. Must be very excitin'—workin' with all them colors and fabrics and all.

JAN [*uneasily*]. It's just a job. [*Changing the subject.*] Rex, have some of this dip.

BRAD [*picking up a cracker daintily*]. I'd love to—thank you. [*Dips it in small dish on table and eats it.*] Ummm! Ain't these tasty!

JAN [*watching him with growing concern*]. Sort of a—delicate taste.

BRAD. Wonder if I could get the recipe. Sure would like to surprise my ma when I go back home!

JAN [*taking a breath*]. Rex—don't you find me attractive?

BRAD [*fighting down amusement*]. Why, yes, ma'am, of course.

JAN. Then why haven't you ever——

BRAD [*as she hesitates*]. Ever what?

JAN. I'm—I'm sorry. I feel so foolish.

BRAD [*earnestly*]. Now go ahead. What's on your mind?

JAN. Well, in all the times we've been going out together——

BRAD. Um-hm?

JAN. You've been a perfect gentleman.

BRAD [*soberly*]. Oh, I hope I have, ma'am.

JAN. Oh, you have. Oh, and I appreciate it, Rex. I really do! But——

BRAD. Yes?

JAN. Well, being a perfect gentleman and all, it's—it's—well, it's not very flattering to me.

BRAD. Well—ma'am. I—I wouldn't want to do anything that might spoil our friendship.

JAN [*disappointed*]. Is that all it is with us—friendship?

BRAD [*firmly*]. Ma'am, that's a direct question. I think it deserves a direct answer. [BRAD *leans forward and kisses* JAN *with authority. As he finishes,* JAN *gasps for air.*]

JAN [*with hushed enthusiasm*]. That's hitting the moon with the first shot!

BRAD. Remember when I said bein' near you was like bein' near a stove on a frosty mornin'?

JAN. Yes.

BRAD. I was wrong—more like a forest fire!

JAN [*shook up, as she looks at him with utter admiration*]. And I was right! [*Getting up, nervously.*] Will you excuse me? I'd better go to the powder moon—I mean room—and fix my lipstick.

BRAD [*has risen with her*]. Hurry back.

JAN [*hushed*]. Don't worry. [*She gives his arm a pat of complete approval, and then moves off* R, *jauntily.*]

[GRAHAM *and* JONATHAN *are coming in* L.]

BRAD [*as he sits again, shocked with his own reaction; to himself*]. What hit me? [*Stares front with surprise, then, talking to himself.*] Brad, boy—the forest fire's getting out of control. It could burn down that big tree standing there all by itself. [GRAHAM *has stopped* JONATHAN *and nodded toward* BRAD.]

GRAHAM. There's our man.

JONATHAN [*sourly*]. With the idiotic expression. I see him. [*Dismissing* GRAHAM.] I can handle it from here. [GRAHAM *goes off* L, *while* JONATHAN *circles to behind* BRAD, *who continues to stare off happily.*]

BRAD [*enjoying a little joke on himself, softly*]. Timber! [JONATHAN *is now standing directly behind the seated* BRAD.]

JONATHAN [*tapping* BRAD'S *shoulder*]. Waiting for someone, cowboy?

BRAD [*without turning, wincing*]. Jonathan Forbes?

JONATHAN [*pleasantly*]. That's right. Just sayin' howdy to my best friend.

BRAD [*still looking forward, earnestly*]. You see, Jonathan—it *started* as a sort of a joke.

JONATHAN. And that's how it's ending. When are you headin' back to the range, Mr. Stetson?

BRAD [*with a sigh*]. Mr. Stetson . . . [*Turns to look at* JONA-

THAN.] I guess that's up to you, isn't it?

JONATHAN. You've got two minutes. We'll do this nice and clean so no one's embarrassed. When she gets back, you'll say you have to leave for some reason, I'll offer to drive her home —and you'll never see her again.

[JAN *is coming back in from* R.]

BRAD. Looks like I haven't much choice.

JONATHAN. Sure looks like it! [JAN *is coming up to them.*]

JAN [*surprised*]. Why, Jonathan! Jonathan, I'd like you to meet——

JONATHAN. We've already met.

JAN [*pleased*]. Well, isn't this nice!

BRAD. Ma'am—I'm sure gonna miss you—leavin' New York and all.

JAN [*thunderstruck*]. You're leaving? When?

BRAD. Tonight.

JONATHAN. In fact—immediately.

BRAD [*uneasily*]. You see, something's come up.

JONATHAN. It's lucky I'm here. I can see you home.

JAN [*heartbroken*]. But you can't just leave! Why, Rex—if you go—I—I'll——

BRAD [*equally unhappy*]. I don't want to go, but——

JONATHAN [*putting in*]. Something came up.

BRAD. Yes, and—and there's just no way I could refuse. [TONY *and* MARIE *have risen from their table and are crossing toward them.*]

JAN. But where will you be? I'll want to write—or maybe I could come, too. [*Almost a cry.*] Rex!

MARIE [*surprised to see him*]. Bradley!

JONATHAN [*wincing*]. Oh, dear.

TONY. Hello, there. Jan, baby—this is Marie.

JAN [*bewildered*]. Hello——

MARIE. You were right, Bradley—Tony *is* interested in show business.

TONY [*to* MARIE]. Come on—you have to get back to the Copa.

MARIE [*going* L *with* TONY]. Don't forget to call, Brad, sweetie.

JAN [*utterly confused*]. Brad?

JONATHAN [*with a shrug*]. You might as well know—his name isn't Rex Stetson.

JAN [*to* BRAD]. It isn't?

JONATHAN. *He's* Brad Allen.

BRAD [*soberly*]. Ma'am—I mean, Miss Morrow—Jan. It sort of got started as a game—because of the telephone business—but I want you to know——

JAN [*hushed*]. How *could* you?

BRAD [*insisting*]. I want you to know that——

JAN. *You're* Brad Allen.

JONATHAN. A sneaking, double-crossing rat!

JAN [*to* JONATHAN]. You said you'd see me home. [*At the point of tears.*] Please—take me home.

BRAD [*after them*]. Jan——

JAN [*pausing to look back*]. It was a *very* good joke. No wonder you're so popular!

BRAD [*unhappily*]. I'll be seeing you, Jan.

JAN [*going*]. Good-by, Mr. Allen. [BRAD *watches them go, and then sits at the small table again. Everyone else is gone and he's alone. He looks back in the direction Jan has gone, and he takes a breath, unhappily. The lights are starting to dim.*]

BRAD [*speaking softly in the direction she went, with determination*]. Be seeing you——[*The lights go out.*]

END OF ACT TWO

ACT THREE

THE CURTAIN RISES, *revealing the two apartments.* BRAD *is sitting alone in his apartment playing a very unsatisfactory game of solitaire on the coffee table in front of the love seat.* ALMA, *in the other apartment, is busy with a can of spray cleaner and a rag and she's as bored with her work as* BRAD *is with his game.*]

BRAD [*dropping remainder of cards on coffee table, disgusted*]. Can't even win at solitaire! [ALMA's *cleaning has brought her close to the telephone, which she notices and then considers.* BRAD *turns to consider telephone, then decides not to call. He shakes his head, gets up, and starts slipping into a sport coat which was over the back of a chair, and fixing his tie.* ALMA, *overcome by curiosity, reaches out cautiously, lifts the receiver with practiced gentleness, and holds her hand over the mouthpiece as she raises it to her ear. Her expression is one of keen anticipation, followed by abrupt disappointment as there's no one on. She drops the telephone back onto the cradle.*]

ALMA [*with a sigh*]. No more party on this line. [ALMA *starts picking up her cleaning things again, but is interrupted by a knock on the door* L.] Just a minute—coming! [BRAD, *having made ready, leaves his apartment, going out* R. ALMA *opens door and speaks to someone outside.*] You're *always* early.

[JONATHAN *comes in, carrying a small bouquet of flowers wrapped in tissue paper.*]

JONATHAN. I could give you the psychological explanation, but——[*His smile suggests she couldn't possibly understand.*] It's complicated.
ALMA. A fear of rejection makes you over-compensate?
JONATHAN [*irked*]. Yes. Jan home yet?

ALMA. Any minute. She said you were coming for dinner.

JONATHAN [*hesitating*]. She—all right?

ALMA [*noncommittal*]. Just like she used to be—putting all her energy into the interior decorating business.

JONATHAN [*concerned*]. The night I brought her home, she was crying so hard I was afraid she'd go to pieces.

ALMA [*defensively*]. Anyone can get the sniffles.

JONATHAN. Sniffles? [*With wonder.*] I never knew a woman that size had that much water in her!

ALMA [*sharply*]. She's perfectly fine! [*Turning.*] I have to put the potatoes in the oven.

JONATHAN [*anxiously*]. Listen, I'm *glad* she's fine—overjoyed! [*Handing over bouquet.*] Here—these are for the table.

ALMA [*taking flowers and starting out U L*]. Make yourself at home.

JONATHAN [*as she goes*]. I'll read something, or put on some records. [*Calling after her. A happy recollection.*] You should've seen the look she gave Brad Allen! Would've frozen an active volcano! [*Noticing small record rack by desk. More to himself.*] Hmm—got some *new* records. [*Picks up album casually as he shouts back to ALMA.*] He couldn't believe he was finished! He couldn't *believe* someone was actually walking out on the great——[*Stops himself as title of record album registers. In lower voice.*] Brad Allen. [*Picks up another album and reads title.*] "Encores of Brad Allen Hits." [*The next album.*] "Instrumental Music from Brad Allen Musicals." [*He crosses toward door U L, carrying records.*] Alma——

ALMA [*calling back*]. I'm busy. [*There is a knock on the door.*]

JONATHAN [*waving albums, demanding*]. I'd like to know how it happens——

ALMA [*calling*]. Would you please answer the door?

JONATHAN. Answer the door——[*Muttering as he crosses to door.*] I'm reduced to that.

[*He opens the door, and* BRAD *comes in.*]

BRAD. Hello, I——Jonathan!

JONATHAN [*concealing records behind him*]. Oh, now, look
. . . I knew you had no shame, but——

BRAD. Is she here?

JONATHAN. No. Why don't you do the decent thing for a
change? Go home, go back to work.

BRAD. I can't work. I just sit at the piano—feeling guilty.

JONATHAN. Guilty? *You?*

BRAD. It's possible.

JONATHAN. I saw you string along three sisters at the same
time! And you came up with some of your best songs. All of
a sudden *one* girl makes you feel guilty. Why?

BRAD. I don't know—but I do!

JONATHAN [*enjoying this*]. Whatta you know? You're in love!
The mighty tree has been toppled! For years I've been waiting
to hear them yell "timber" over you!

BRAD [*soberly*]. Maybe I'm hearing it, too. Maybe you're right.

JONATHAN. You're darn right I'm right!

BRAD. Has Jan—has she said anything?

JONATHAN. I haven't seen her since the night I took her home.

BRAD. Well, *that* night—on the way home—did she give any
indication?

JONATHAN. *Beyond* what she said to your face?

BRAD. I mean, was there anything that might lead you to
think——

JONATHAN. Calm, cool, collected——

BRAD. But I thought——

JONATHAN. A little embarrassed, that's all—but she got right
over it. The only thing on her mind now is the interior
decorating business. [*With this,* JONATHAN *turns and puts
the records back on the rack.*]

BRAD. You're sure?

JONATHAN. I can't tell you how much I'm enjoying this. You
love her—and she can't stand the sight of you.

BRAD [*determined*]. Jonathan—*how* do I get her back?

JONATHAN. You don't. That's the beauty of it! You suffer—
and I watch!

BRAD. But there's a way! There's *got* to be a way.

JONATHAN. It's a delightful situation. The great Brad Allen chopped down to size! Floating down the river with the rest of us logs.

BRAD [*trying hard to think this out*]. When you want to get on friendly terms with a girl, you're—you're nice to her dog.

JONATHAN. No dog.

BRAD. If there's no dog, then you're nice to her mother.

JONATHAN. Milwaukee, Wisconsin.

BRAD. If worse comes to worst, you work on her maid.

JONATHAN. Alma? You couldn't get to first base with her.

BRAD [*quietly registering*]. Alma. [*To* JONATHAN.] Thanks a lot. [*Calling.*] Alma!

[ALMA, *holding a vase and the unwrapped bouquet in her hand, steps in* U L. *It's evident that she's been just outside the door.*]

ALMA [*regarding* BRAD *with big eyes*]. Yes?

BRAD. Excuse me—may I talk to you?

ALMA. Sure.

BRAD [*coming over, all charm*]. My name is Brad Allen. [*He takes flowers and puts them in vase.*] And I, uh—I——

ALMA. I know you. I'd know that voice of yours anywhere.

BRAD. You know me?

ALMA [*humming melody line* BRAD *was singing earlier, ending with the names*]. Eileen—Yvette.

BRAD. The—party line?

ALMA. I'm one of your most devoted listeners.

BRAD. Why, thank you, dear.

JONATHAN [*sharply*]. Alma!

ALMA [*to* JONATHAN, *pained*]. Please——

JONATHAN. All he's trying to do is——

ALMA [*cutting in*]. Work on me. Get on my good side—I know. [*To* BRAD.] Go ahead.

BRAD. Maybe it's crazy coming over here, but I've *got* to do something!

ALMA. Let's take this from the beginning. First—you're in love
with her?

BRAD. Yes.

ALMA. And you wanta win her back?

BRAD. Right.

JONATHAN [*outraged*]. Will you stop this?

ALMA [*ignoring* JONATHAN]. The way I see your problem,
you have to get her to talk to you, right?

BRAD. You're infallible.

ALMA. It's very simple. All you have to do——

JONATHAN. Cut it out!

ALMA. I just wanted to explain that——

JONATHAN. Now *stop*.

ALMA [*persisting*]. The simple solution is to——[*Hesitates as
she hears someone at the door* L, *toward which she looks.*]
And—well——

[JAN, *carrying her brief case, comes in* L.]

ALMA [*closing the subject*]. It's a simple solution. [*To* JAN.]
Just talking about you. [*Embarrassed.*] What I mean——
[*Changing subject.*] Anyway—the potatoes are in the oven.
[JAN *is quietly surveying the scene.*]

JONATHAN [*to* JAN, *smiling*]. I'm always early—over-com-
pensation.

BRAD [*to* JAN, *in a low voice*]. Hello, Jan.

ALMA [*putting in*]. I made a nice salad.

JAN. Good evening, Jonathan. Am I interrupting?

JONATHAN. Not me.

ALMA. And the table's all set, except for——[*She holds out
flowers.*]

JONATHAN. I brought them.

JAN [*taking vase*]. How lovely.

BRAD. Jan—please.

JAN [*to* ALMA]. I'll have to step out and admire all you've
done.

BRAD [*urgently*]. Wait—Jan. Look, I don't blame you for hating me! But I'm trying to apologize.

JAN [*going*]. Excuse me.

BRAD [*calling*]. If you'd just let me——[*But she has gone out* U L.]

JONATHAN [*in a soft voice, taunting*]. Like Alma was saying —it's very simple.

BRAD [*a plea*]. If you've got an idea, Alma—tell me.

ALMA [*hushed*]. I'm not sure if it'll work—but you've got an apartment. She decorates apartments. You hire her to do your place. Two people, decorating an apartment, that's—pretty intimate.

JONATHAN [*also hushed*]. Shame——

ALMA [*a whisper*]. She'd *have* to talk to you. Clever?

BRAD [*whispering back*]. Clever.

JONATHAN [*bitterly*]. There should be someone or something I could report you to!

BRAD [*also to* ALMA]. If anything comes of this—I'll put you in a song.

ALMA. You mean? . . . [*Gives melody line, then with her name.*] *Alma?*

BRAD. Right! [*There is a rap on the door* L, *and* ALMA *crosses to it.*]

ALMA [*bubbling*]. Gee—this is like *old* times!

JONATHAN. You're out of your minds. She won't decorate your apartment! She despises you! Didn't you just see her? She won't even *talk* to you!

[ALMA *opens door and* PIEROT *hurries in.*]

PIEROT. Miss Morrow back yet? Another one of those Scarsdale jobs came through.

ALMA. She just came in. [*To* BRAD, *pointedly.*] Mr. Pierot is in the decorating business *with* her.

BRAD [*coming forward with his hand out*]. My name's Brad Allen. [*Shaking hands.*] And I have an urgent decorating problem.

PIEROT. Well, that's our business, and we're always happy——

BRAD. The place I want decorated is only a few steps from here. If you could take a moment now——

ALMA [to PIEROT]. Might as well tend to business. [*Gestures back* U L.] She'll be starting dinner, anyway.

JONATHAN [*between his teeth, to* ALMA]. Collaborationist!

PIEROT [*starting* U L]. Just let me speak to——

BRAD [*grabbing his arm and swinging him around*]. Understand this—I want a *complete* redecorating! [*As though joking.*] You see, I'm changing my whole way of life.

JONATHAN [*this is ridiculous*]. Now, hold on a minute——

BRAD [*going right on to* PIEROT]. Your company shouldn't pass up a job like this. [*He opens the door* L.] Since Miss Morrow can't talk to me right now, maybe I can get things started with you.

PIEROT. Well, if it's just a few steps from here——[*To* ALMA.] Tell her I'll phone later.

ALMA [*pleasantly*]. No hurry. [PIEROT *is going out* L, *followed by* BRAD.]

BRAD. Just a few details to work out on how the job is to be handled. [*They complete exit* L.]

JONATHAN [*he could kill* ALMA]. If I thought there was the slightest chance anything could come of your treachery, your knife in the back, your perfidious——

[JAN *has come in* U L *and she stands quietly in the doorway.*]

JAN. It's all right, Jonathan.

JONATHAN. Oh, sure—meanwhile he's working out the details! [*Furious.*] Jan—do you know what he's up to now?

JAN [*giving a slight nod*]. I heard. I'm getting as bad as Alma.

ALMA [*clearing her throat*]. There's still time for me to put an ad in the Sunday paper: Meddlesome housekeeper wants situation.

JAN [*gesturing toward kitchen*]. You forgot to defrost the refrigerator.

ALMA [*muttering, as she goes*]. Pick, pick, pick. [*The moment* ALMA *goes out* U L, JAN'S *reserve begins to break.*]

JAN [*hurt and unhappy*]. Jonathan . . . why would *any* man
talk like that? It's just horrible! And all he cares about now
is working out some cute scheme for getting me back in line
with the rest of his girls!

JONATHAN. With your trusted Alma making a great little
accomplice.

JAN [*incredulous*]. But the gall of the man—coming *here* to
plan his next move! It's—it's monstrous!

JONATHAN. Put it out of your mind, Jan.

JAN. I can't! [*Clenching her fists, vehemently.*] If there was
just some way I could get back at him—some way to make
him feel the humiliation, and—and the disappointment, and
——[*She's interrupted by the telephone's ringing. She turns
and stares at it as though the telephone had suddenly turned
into a live cobra.*]

ALMA [*from kitchen*]. Shall *I* answer it?

JAN [*calling back*]. No. Never mind.

JONATHAN. If it's him, why don't you pass along these com-
ments?

JAN [*deciding*]. Maybe I will——[*Picking up telephone,
sharply.*] Yes—what is it?

[PIEROT *is stepping on* D R, *holding a telephone in his hand.*]

PIEROT. Hello, Jan—it's Pierot. [*As she hesitates.*] *Pierot!*

JAN. Pierot? [*Still on edge.*] Where are you calling from?

PIEROT. I stopped at a phone booth. [*Firmly.*] Jan, we have to
tell Mr. Allen to get some other decorator to do his apartment.

JAN [*surprised*]. You're turning him down?

PIEROT. Absolutely. I have to.

JAN. I see. [*Curiously.*] What—what made you decide?

PIEROT [*with a suggestion of indignation*]. I found out this is
a *personal* matter—and I gather what *your* attitude is about
him!

JAN. But, specifically—what did he——

PIEROT. When he went on to say he'd only trust *you* with the
job, I could see what he was up to. I told him it was out of the
question.

JAN [*a statement rather than a question, considering*]. He said he'd *trust* me with the job?

PIEROT. In view of the personal aspect, I gave him a flat no!

JAN [*thoughtfully*]. Now, wait a minute . . . I'm trying to think. For one thing I don't want us to lose a good commission because of *my* personal feelings.

PIEROT [*grandly*]. Jan—I *refuse* to subject you to an experience that might be—how would you say it—traumatic!

JAN. Now, that's silly. Look—once I had the mumps. It wasn't very pleasant, but I got over it.

PIEROT [*puzzled*]. The *mumps?*

JAN. I look upon Brad Allen like any other disease! I've had him—it's over—I'm immune to him!

JONATHAN [*feeling a faint stir of apprehension*]. Careful, now . . .

PIEROT [*still holding back*]. But are you *positive?*

JAN. Completely.

PIEROT [*giving in, but still doubtful*]. Well, if you think you can handle it——

JAN. I certainly can!

PIEROT [*washing his hands of it*]. It's *your* decision.

JAN [*with growing authority*]. Get back to Mr. Allen—tell him I'm dropping everything. I'll be right over.

JONATHAN [*his apprehension growing*]. Don't be crazy!

PIEROT [*sounding as apprehensive as* JONATHAN]. But what for? You're rushing things.

JAN [*parroting* BRAD'S *earlier comment*]. Just a few details to work out on how the job's to be handled. [*She hangs up; and then drums her fingers on the top of the telephone. Her expression is one of fast calculation.* JONATHAN *winces and turns away.*]

JONATHAN [*half to himself, hushed*]. Oh, no . . . no! [PIEROT *has taken the telephone from his ear, and his hands drop to his side, still holding the receiver. The energy seems to drain out of him.*]

PIEROT [*taking a breath, and facing offstage* R]. All right, Mr. Allen——

[BRAD *strolls on* R, *crossing behind* PIEROT, *who looks back nervously over his head.*]

PIEROT [*defensively*]. I told her *exactly* what you said.

BRAD. I know. I was listening. [*Demanding.*] Well?

PIEROT. She's coming right over. [*Bewildered.*] But I don't know why. I mean, the way you had me put it.

BRAD. Because she'd have turned down any other approach. [*More to himself; hushed.*] And when you're fighting for your life, you've *got* to get smart.

PIEROT [*hesitant*]. Mr. Allen——If I *hadn't* told her what you said——[*Embarrassed.*] Were you going to beat me up?

BRAD. The business associate of the girl I love? [*As they go off* R.] You must've misunderstood. [*In the other apartment,* JONATHAN *has turned back to* JAN, *whom he is regarding critically.*]

JONATHAN. I think you're out of your mind! [*As she continues to drum with her fingers, looking off into space.*] What are you trying to do? Send a message in code?

JAN [*coming to a focus on* JONATHAN *again*]. Don't you see? This gives me a chance to even things up a little!

JONATHAN [*flatly*]. No, I *don't* see.

JAN [*eagerly*]. Oh, I can't wait to get started! Would you walk me over to his place? Around the back, it should be even closer.

JONATHAN. Sure, I'll walk you, but I still don't see.

JAN [*crossing to door* L, *impatiently*]. He has his hilarious Rex Stetson story—probably making him the life of every party!

JONATHAN [*opening door* L]. So you want to give him *another* story.

JAN. No.

[ALMA *has come to the kitchen door* U L.]

ALMA. Say—before you go over there——

JONATHAN [*to* JAN, *caustically*]. The acoustics in this apartment must be wonderful.

ALMA [*wounded*]. All I wanted to ask—what about the dinner?
JAN. I'm afraid you'll have to eat it yourself. [*To* JONATHAN.]
Come along. [JAN *goes out* L. JONATHAN *gives* ALMA *a final glare and follows her.*]
ALMA [*looking after them; as though in retort, giving Brad's melody line, then adding the name*]. *Jan!* [ALMA *nods with satisfaction at her little joke and goes back into the kitchen.*]

[BRAD, *meanwhile, comes into his apartment, where he hurries to get everything in order for Jan's arrival.* JAN *and* JONATHAN *come on* D L *and start crossing* R *in front of the apartments.*]

JONATHAN [*taking hold of her arm to stop her*]. Jan—before you get there——Have you got some rational plan?
JAN. Yes! [*Speaking carefully.*] The spider wants me to redecorate his web——[*Starting* R *again.*] Now, doesn't that open up some exciting possibilities?
JONATHAN [*still standing there, blankly*]. I haven't the slightest idea what you——[*Hurrying to catch up with her.*] Jan, don't you want me to come up with you?
JAN [*pausing, shaking her head*]. I have to handle this myself. [*Reassuring.*] But you'll be in on the rest of it! [*As they start* R *again; with anticipation.*] Maybe we'll come up with a funny story, too! [*She goes off* R.]
JONATHAN [*a happy thought*]. About the ex-Rex! [*As he follows her off* R.] That'd make *me* the life of the party. [JONATHAN *completes exit* R. BRAD *has crossed to his small wall mirror where he makes a quick check as to his appearance. In an attempt at self-encouragement, he holds up his hand to the mirror in the "V for Victory" position.*]
BRAD [*speaking to his reflection*]. Well—good luck. [*As* BRAD *turns, his eye is caught by something down beside the piano, and suddenly he does a "take." He crosses quickly, reaches down and picks up his cowboy hat. He stands hesitating as to what to do with it. There is a knock on his door.* BRAD *is startled, looks about anxiously.*] Just a moment——[*He*

hurries to door U R *and tosses cowboy hat inside, then crosses back to door* R.] Right with you. [BRAD *opens the door. He stands aside, continuing to look out. He speaks soberly.*] Won't you come in, please?

[JAN, *stony-faced, comes in a few steps, stops, and then looks at* BRAD *without expression.*]

BRAD [*a bit uncomfortable*]. I had a preliminary discussion with Mr. Pierot. This apartment—well, it's high time it was re-decorated.

JAN [*repeating*]. High time——[*All business; encouraging him to continue.*] Yes, Mr. Allen?

BRAD. Well, of course, I thought of you—to decorate. But then I thought perhaps——

JAN [*as he hesitates, without expression*]. Go on——

BRAD. It's just that, well—it's a little embarrassing.

JAN [*coldly*]. Mr. Allen, I'm a decorator. You're a client. I'm here because you're paying for my professional services. Now —what style do you have in mind?

BRAD [*uneasily*]. Uuh—n-nothing in particular. [*The solution.*] I'm leaving it entirely up to you.

JAN [*carefully*]. You're sure you want to do that?

BRAD. Oh, yes. I have all the confidence in the world——[*With a winning smile.*] I just want to put myself in your hands.

JAN [*quietly, as though approving a sound business judgment*]. That should make things much easier.

BRAD [*not quite able to make her out*]. Yes, well——[*He turns and gestures.*] This is the way the place is now . . . but then, you've already seen it.

JAN [*a bit shaken in spite of herself*]. Oh, I remember—— [*She has to swallow.*] Such a beautiful view of the park!

BRAD [*considering her now, a bit shaken, too*]. Jan——[*Catching himself.*] I'm sorry. I'll keep this business. [*With sincerity.*] What I'm trying to say, I want you to make this the sort of place that—well—that *you'd* feel comfortable in.

JAN [*almost ready to believe his apparent sincerity*]. You really want—you——

BRAD [*cutting in*]. Why don't you get right started?

JAN. Now?

BRAD. Sure. Go right ahead and take over. [*Crossing to piano.*] And while you're getting organized, I'll be over here doing my work.

JAN [*remembering his scheme*]. And then we'll talk——

BRAD [*casually*]. Well, after all, two people decorating an apartment——

JAN [*all business again*]. I'm sorry, Mr. Allen. If I'm to get started you'll have to move out—and stay away till I've finished.

BRAD [*startled*]. Move out?

JAN. It's the only way I can do the job—and I have something very special in mind. You'd just be in the way.

BRAD. But there might be things that—that you'll want to discuss with me.

JAN. If you want me to do this job, you'll have to give me carte blanche!

BRAD. But I——

JAN. Unless you feel I can't handle it.

BRAD. Oh, no—I'll leave. I'll get some things together—— [*Pointedly.*] I'll move into the Y for a few days.

JAN. The key, please?

BRAD [*taking key out of his pocket*]. You *do* want to fix my apartment?

JAN [*holding out her hand*]. More than anything in the world.

BRAD [*handing her key*]. I'll be out of here tonight. Just do the place the way you'd like it. [*Smiles pleasantly.*] Surprise me.

JAN [*pausing at the door, smiling pleasantly in reply*]. I will. [*At this moment the lights black out.*]

[*In the darkness a telephone is heard ringing, and as the lights come up again,* ALMA *is hurrying in from the kitchen in Jan's apartment to pick up the telephone.*]

ALMA [*into telephone*]. Hello?

[BRAD *steps on* D R, *holding a telephone in his hand.*]

BRAD [*cautiously*]. Alma?

ALMA. Yes?

BRAD. She isn't around, is she? This is Brad.

ALMA. Not now. From the moment she took on your apartment, she's been on the run.

BRAD [*faintly puzzled*]. I wouldn't think it'd be that much of a problem.

ALMA. She doesn't confide in me these days, but I have an idea she's mainly shopping right now—looking into a lot of shops she doesn't usually deal with, too.

BRAD [*pleased*]. Making a special job of it, eh?

ALMA. Must be *extra* special.

BRAD. Great! [*Glowing.*] This scheme didn't start off the way we planned, but it's sure going to end up right!

ALMA. Just so I won't worry—how's that?

BRAD. You'll be shifting down the street to work for both of us!

ALMA [*delighted*]. You mean it?

BRAD [*with fervor*]. I can hardly wait to carry my bride over the threshold! And I carry her into a beautiful redecorated apartment——[*Unable to repress a moment of boastfulness.*] An apartment, incidentally, that'll be *exactly* what she wants! Clever?

ALMA [*conceding*]. Clever! [*The lights black out again. In the darkness* JAN'S *voice is heard calling.*]

JAN [*off* R]. Please—just put the rest of the load in the hall by the door.

MAN [*off* R]. Okay, lady.

JAN [*off* R, *sharply*]. Careful—some of those things are—are irreplaceable!

[*The light comes up on* JAN *and* JONATHAN *coming through the door* R *to Brad's apartment, carrying the most garish and hideous lamps that can be found.*]

JAN [*setting hers down*]. I just hope this is nauseating enough.

JONATHAN [*putting his down*]. Among nauseating lamps—these are collectors' items!

[*Two girl assistants,* TILDA *and* ANN, *are coming in* R *loaded with more horrors in the worst possible taste.* NOTE: *The "redecorating" of the apartment should be carefully rehearsed so that the maximum effect can be achieved in the least possible time. More "assistants" can be added to the cast if desired, but their movements should be planned so they proceed efficiently. Some of the lines that follow can be altered as necessary to suit the particular props to be used in the production. It should be immediately evident, however, with every item brought into the apartment, that* JAN'S *intention is to turn the place into a ghastly example of overwhelming bad taste. If possible, the dominating props to be introduced should be the large, ugly lamps. They should contain strong colored light bulbs, and be hooked up immediately. They should not be turned on, however, until later as specified in the script, at which point the climax of the retaliatory redecoration is achieved.*]

JAN [*to* ANN]. Put the statuary on the piano——[*To* TILDA.] And the throw goes over the love seat.

TILDA [*wincing as she spreads a cheap, garish throw over love seat*]. You can't be serious!

JAN [*firmly*]. There's a lot of work to be done. [TILDA *shrugs and goes out* R *for another load.*]

ANN [*arranging a piece of gilded junk statuary*]. This isn't exactly your usual job!

JAN [*busy rearranging*]. We're not trying to suit ourselves. We suit the client.

JONATHAN [*going out* R]. I'll get the other lamp.

ANN [*curiously, as she works*]. This *suits* the client?

JAN. This is a very unusual client.

ANN [*eying the development of the room*]. I can see that.

[TILDA *is coming back, possibly carrying a brilliant, rainbow-colored rug.*]

TILDA. I just can't believe it!

JAN [*to* TILDA]. In front of the coffee table.

TILDA. This client—I hope he's color blind?

JAN [*grimly*]. You like being one of my assistants?

TILDA [*earnestly*]. Oh, yes, Miss Morrow.

ANN. Me, too.

JAN. Then get on with the assisting! [JONATHAN *calls from outside.*]

JONATHAN [*off* R]. Here I come, ready or not!

[JONATHAN *walks in with a tremendous floor lamp that is by far the worst of all. He stands there, smiling, beside it. The lights black out again.*]

[*In the darkness a telephone is heard ringing. A spot of light comes up* D L *and* EILEEN *steps into it, holding a telephone.*]

EILEEN. Hello? [*A look of delight comes over her face. Enthusiastically:*] Hello, Brad! I haven't heard from you for *days!*

[*Another spot has come up at the other side of the stage* D R *and* BRAD *has come into it, also holding a telephone.*]

BRAD. I've been wanting to call you, Eileen.

EILEEN [*sighing*]. Wonderful to hear your voice again!

BRAD. Eileen, dear. You see, I want you to be the first to know. I've met this girl. I've fallen in love with her—and I'm planning to marry her.

EILEEN [*her face falling*]. I'll die!

BRAD. Nonsense, dear. You have everything to live for!

EILEEN. You can't really mean it.

BRAD. But I do.

EILEEN. Has the date been set?

BRAD. Very soon now.

EILEEN [*demanding*]. How soon?

BRAD. It should be taking place just as soon as my apartment's redecorated. Good-by, Eileen. [*The spots are dimming out.*]

EILEEN [*with a heavy sigh*]. Good-by, Brad. [*The spots are out*

completely. In the darkness there is a sudden cry from
JONATHAN.]
JONATHAN. *Ow!*
JAN. What is it? What's the matter?

[*The lights come up again, and* JONATHAN *and* JAN *are revealed once more in Brad's apartment, which is now well on
its way to being turned into a museum of horrors.* JONATHAN
*is staring indignantly at a ridiculous chair he has just brought
into the apartment.*]

JONATHAN [*to* JAN]. After the struggle to get that chair up
here, I just wanted to rest for a minute.
JAN. But what happened?
JONATHAN [*outraged*]. That chair *bit* me!
JAN. Good.
JONATHAN [*irritated*]. Good?

[ANN *and* TILDA *are coming in loaded down with more out-
standing examples of terrible taste, which they proceed efficiently to place about the apartment.*]

JAN [*continuing to* JONATHAN, *contrite*]. I'm sorry if it bit
you, Jonathan, but——
JONATHAN [*offended*]. Well, thanks——
TILDA [*to* JAN]. You want this over here?
JAN. It fits the general scheme.
ANN. Looks like we cleaned out the concessions at Coney Island.
TILDA. I'm beginning to get used to the stuff. [*Shaking head.*]
Isn't *that* a frightening thought!
ANN. I'll say one thing—it's a change.
JAN [*to girls*]. Never mind the commentary.
JONATHAN [*who has been putting chair into position, to* JAN].
About here?
JAN. That's fine, Jonathan. [*Explaining.*] All I meant before
——I guess I was visualizing the moment when his majesty
mounts this throne. [*Enjoying her vision.*] Can't you just
see it!

JONATHAN [*visualizing*]. Yeah.
JAN. Well, how does it strike you?
JONATHAN [*still seeing it, decisively*]. *Good!*
JAN [*her point proven*]. Good.

[*The lights black out again, and in the darkness a telephone is heard ringing. A spot of light comes up D L, and YVETTE steps into it, holding a telephone.*]

YVETTE. Yes? [*Then, with shock.*] No!

[*Another spot of light is coming up again D R, into which BRAD steps, also holding a telephone.*]

BRAD [*insisting*]. Yes. It's me, all right—Brad.
YVETTE. Where have you been, *cherie?*
BRAD. Well, that's what I wanted to explain.
YVETTE [*admiring*]. You always explain so beautifully.
BRAD. Yvette—I wanted you to be the first to know. I've met this girl—and we're about to be married.
YVETTE [*making sure*]. This is Brad—Brad Allen?
BRAD. Surprising how things can change. . . . Even my old apartment—completely redecorated. The big unveiling is to-night. I'd ask you over, but it's just going to be—well—*family.* [*The spots of light go out on this. In the darkness, a telephone operator's voice is heard.*]
OPERATOR [*speaking mechanically*]. At the tone the time will be 8:00 p.m.—exactly. [*This is followed by a single beep.*]

[*The lights are coming up during this, revealing JONATHAN holding the telephone in Jan's apartment. JAN is sitting on the sofa, and ALMA is standing in the kitchen doorway drying some dishes.*]

JONATHAN [*hanging up*]. If Pierot is on schedule, they're walking into the apartment right now.
JAN. We should've gone, too.

JONATHAN. You mean, return to the scene of the crime?

JAN [*shrugging*]. *We* committed it!

JONATHAN. Poor old Brad! I hope he hasn't thrown away his phone numbers. He's gonna need a lot of consoling.

JAN [*casually*]. Why would he throw away his phone numbers?

ALMA [*from doorway*]. Because maybe he fell in love with someone.

JAN [*scornfully*]. Brad Allen!

JONATHAN [*delighted*]. That's what makes it so great! This time *he's* the one that did the falling!

JAN. But he could no more——

JONATHAN [*cutting in*]. But he *did!* I could hardly believe it— the great Brad Allen in love!

JAN [*quietly*]. You're not serious.

JONATHAN [*emphatically*]. Sure, I am. And when you gave him what he had coming, it *really* got him!

JAN. But how do you know?

JONATHAN [*with satisfaction*]. Ever since I went through college with the guy, I've been waiting to see him on the hook like this.

JAN [*pressing*]. Jonathan . . . what are you saying?

ALMA [*putting in again*]. That the man's in love with you.

JONATHAN. Right.

JAN [*an incredulous whisper*]. Right?

ALMA. So he was trying to find some way to win you back.

JONATHAN [*almost gloating*]. And wait'll he sees how it all turned out!

ALMA [*to JAN, with mock cheerfulness*]. You're having the last laugh on him, all right.

JONATHAN [*agreeing eagerly*]. He'll be walking into that apartment expecting to see the work of a woman in love!

JAN [*utterly crushed*]. Yes, and . . . and that's exactly . . . [*She turns away, hiding her face in the sofa.*]

JONATHAN [*startled*]. Jan!

ALMA. Leave her alone for a minute.

JONATHAN. But what in the world is she——

ALMA [*gesturing for him to come*]. There's about one cup of coffee left. We'll split it.

JONATHAN [*concerned*]. Jan?

JAN [*without turning, keeping control of her voice*]. I'll be fine—in a minute. [ALMA *gestures again for him to come.*]

JONATHAN [*starting for kitchen, trying to sort it out*]. We're enjoying a great big last laugh—then all at once she's crying into the sofa.

ALMA [*casually*]. That's what they call the female prerogative.

JONATHAN [*as he goes out*]. I may need *all* that coffee. [ALMA *follows* JONATHAN *out* U L.]

[*The door to Brad's apartment is opened and* PIEROT *hurries in. He pushes the door almost shut behind him, calling back out the remaining crack.*]

PIEROT. You're to wait just a moment—I'm following instructions.

BRAD [*off* R]. Come on—hurry. [PIEROT *turns, and the ghastly appearance of the room almost floors him. With an expression of acute discomfort on his face he snaps on the lamps. Their colored light bulbs add a garish illumination and thus the crowning touch to the scene.*]

PIEROT [*a dispirited call*]. All right——

[BRAD *pushes the door open wide, and steps eagerly inside.*]

BRAD [*all expectation*]. Just let me—[*Finishing mechanically.*] —have a look. [*His expression freezes into a set grimace. His voice now is quiet.*] Oh . . . I see. [*He continues his inspection.*] Yes. . . .

PIEROT [*edging toward door*]. If you'll excuse me . . . actually I didn't . . . well, this wasn't *my* job.

BRAD [*deadly calm*]. No—it was Miss Morrow. I insisted.

PIEROT. You'll excuse me . . . [PIEROT *slides out the door* R. BRAD *turns back to survey the room again, and as he does, a drum roll is begun quietly offstage and begins to increase in volume. The fast rat-tat-tat of the drum reaches a climax.*

BRAD *takes a deep breath, sets his jaw grimly, and starts out the door. The drum roll changes to a marching beat.* BRAD *goes out his apartment door* R, *is unseen for a moment as the drum beat continues, then comes on* D R, *striding across the stage in time to the beat, and goes off* L. *The drum beat continues for a moment, then stops. As soon as it does, there is a sharp knock on Jan's door.* JAN *looks up startled, wiping her eyes.*]

[*The door* L *is pushed open and* BRAD *strides in.*]

JAN. What are you doing here?
BRAD. I want to show you something.
JAN. What?
BRAD. My apartment.
JAN. I've seen it.
BRAD. You'll see it again.
JAN [*starting for kitchen*]. I'll do nothing of the kind.
BRAD. Oh, yes, you will!

[ALMA *comes to kitchen door.*]

JAN [*to* ALMA, *who is blocking way*]. Let me through——
ALMA [*to* JAN]. You don't want to run away.
JAN. Alma!
JONATHAN [*off* U L, *calling*]. What's going on?
BRAD [*to* JAN]. If this has to be by force . . .
JAN [*backing toward the sofa again*]. You wouldn't dare!
BRAD [*continuing to approach*]. You've been wrong about me before, you know.

[JONATHAN, *muttering to himself, manages to push in past* ALMA.]

JAN [*stepping up onto the sofa to get away*]. Don't touch me!
  [*The drum roll begins again.*]
BRAD [*warning*]. Jan——
JAN. I'll scream!

JONATHAN. Now, stop this——[*The drum roll is building.*]

BRAD [*to* JAN]. Are you coming?

JAN. No.

BRAD. Yes! [*He stoops, throws her over his shoulder fireman-fashion, and turns toward the door.*]

JAN [*a cry*]. Brad—put me down!

JONATHAN. If you don't put her down——[*The drum roll reaches a climax.*]

BRAD [*shouting*]. Open the door!

ALMA [*rushing to do so, delighted*]. Yes, sir! [*The drum starts beating out a march, as* BRAD *strides out the door* L *with the protesting* JAN *over his shoulder.* JONATHAN *scurries out after them.*]

JONATHAN. You're crazy! You're out of your mind!

[*They are out the door* L *and lost from view for a moment. Then* JONATHAN *rushes on* D L, *and hurries across to* R.]

JONATHAN. Help! Officer! Police!

[BRAD *comes striding on* L *in time to the drum beat, and is crossing* R.]

JAN [*furiously*]. Put me down! Oh, put me down! Please——

[*The* POLICEMAN *seen in the first act is strolling on from* R, *and* JONATHAN *hurries up to him.*]

JONATHAN. Officer—you're just in time. [*Gestures.*] I want you to arrest this man.

JAN. He won't put me down!

POLICEMAN. This the girl you were telling me about, Brad?

BRAD. That's right, Kelly.

POLICEMAN [*with appreciation, starting on again* L, *leaving them*]. Can't say as I blame you.

JONATHAN [*incredulous*]. But . . . officer . . .

BRAD [*resuming march*]. This way, Miss Morrow——[*He*

carries her off R, *followed helplessly by* JONATHAN. *They're out of sight for a brief moment. Then the drum beats out another roll and stops.*]

[BRAD *walks into his apartment through the door* R, *carrying* JAN.]

JAN. All right—you've got me up to see the stupid mess I made. Now, will you kindly put me down?

BRAD [*doing so gently*]. Sure. It's just customary for the groom to carry the bride across the threshold.

JAN. What bride?

BRAD [*indicating the room*]. I suppose you feel pretty cute about this?

JAN. *What* bride?

BRAD [*raging*]. You don't know? Why did I spend a fortune having this apartment done over? Why did I cut myself off from every girl I know? Why does any man destroy himself? Because he thinks he's getting married! And what does it get me?

JAN. What you were saying about a bride——

BRAD [*shaking lamp at her*]. This is what it gets me! [*As he looks at it, his rage gives way to amusement.*] Maybe we should leave it this way.

JAN [*horrified*]. Oh, no——

BRAD [*amused*]. We might be able to charge admission.

[JONATHAN *is coming in* R.]

JAN. You're going to see the fastest re-decoration.

JONATHAN [*surprised again*]. How could you *not* be fighting? What's going on?

BRAD. A wedding—only this time you're going to be the best man.

JONATHAN [*smiling wryly*]. It's a change, anyway. With me it's been always a bridegroom, never a best man.

JAN [*radiant*]. I just can't believe it! [*Sinking down onto the chair.*] I'm just so happy I could——[*She leaps up from the chair with a shriek.*] *Ow!*

BRAD [*his arms around her, startled*]. What is it? What happened? [*The curtain is falling.*]

JAN [*pointing back at the chair*]. It *bit* me!

THE CURTAIN IS DOWN

WHAT PEOPLE ARE SAYING about *Pillow Talk*...

"Play was great and the audience fell in love with all of the characters. This was NOT your average high-school production."

Reginald Peters, DeSoto High School,
DeSoto, Texas

"*Pillow Talk* was a delightful movie, but it is even more delightful as a stage play. It is incredibly fun to stage. Actors love it, and audiences adore it. It is so difficult to find shows appropriate for the whole family, and this one is!"   *Sherry Smith,*
Cyprus High School, Magna, Utah

"A great high-school production with a lot of acting opportunities and a fun, lighthearted subject. Our audiences loved it."

Kathleen Switzer, El Dorado High School,
Placentia, Calif.

"*Pillow Talk* is a wonderful adaptation from the screenplay! This was my favorite production that I have done with my after-school program."   *Christa Jones,*
Ocean Lakes High School, Virginia Beach, Va.

"One of the favorite plays by cast and crew!"

Steven Allar, Auburndale High School,
Auburndale, Wis.

"Our drama troupe found *Pillow Talk* to be a delightful show. One basic set was easy to build while special scenes gave the backstage crew something to keep them busy. The actors enjoyed delving into the personalities of the characters. The audience went away smiling. What more could we ask?"

Margie Thomson, Ida High School,
Ida, Mich.